FINANCIAL MANAGEMENT 101:

Get a Grip on Your Business Numbers

FINANCIAL MANAGEMENT 101:
Get a Grip on Your Business Numbers

Angie Mohr, CA, CMA

Self-Counsel Press
(a division of)
International Self-Counsel Press
USA   Canada

Self-Counsel Press acknowledges the financial support of the Government of Canada through the Book Publishing Industry Development Program (BPIDP) for our publishing activities.

Printed in Canada.

First edition: 2003

Cataloguing in Publication Data

Mohr, Angie
    Financial Management 101: Get a Grip on Your Business Numbers
/ Angie Mohr. — 1st ed.(Self-counsel business series)

   (Self-counsel business series)
   Includes bibliographical references

   ISBN   1-55180-448-4

   1. Small business—Finance. 2. Small business — Management 3. Accounting. I. Title. II. Series
HG4027.7. M63 2003   657'. 9042 C2003-911181-4

Self-Counsel Press
(a division of)
International Self-Counsel Press Ltd.

1704 N. State Street	1481 Charlotte Road
Bellingham, WA 98225	North Vancouver, BC V7J 1H1
USA	Canada

Contents

Samples

Diagrams

Tables

Worksheet

NOTICE TO READERS

Laws are constantly changing. Every effort is made to keep this publication as current as possible. However, the author, the publisher, and the vendor of this book make no representation or warranties regarding the outcome or the use to which the information in this book is put and are not assuming any liability for any claims, losses, or damages arising out of the use of this book. The reader should not rely on the author or the publisher of this book for any professional advice. Please be sure that you have the most recent edition.

Acknowledgments

Books are never a solo effort. I wish to thank the following people for their assistance, guidance, and moral support, without which this book would most likely still be a pile of papers stacked on my desk:

- The team at Mohr & Company: April, Tim, Lindsay, and Yesenia
- Richard Day, Judy Brunsek, and the great group at Self-Counsel Press
- Hayley Chandler, Dave Sturgeon, John Weir, and Andrew Pyper for their encouragement and the occasional beer
- All my clients who participated in the development of this series
- My family for their support
- And last, but most important, my husband, Jeff, for all his help and for believing in the project

Introduction

Small businesses are the engine of the North American economy, and people like Joe and Becky (our case study), with no formal business training, run most small businesses. Many business owners believe that bookkeeping software like *Simply Accounting* and *QuickBooks* will magically prepare and analyze financial information for them. Because the owners lack basic accounting skills, they are unable to analyze their business results and have no idea what's working and what's not. These businesses tend to languish and eventually die from neglect of analysis.

Financial Management 101: Get a Grip On Your Business Numbers is the second book in the Self-Counsel Press *Numbers 101* series aimed at small business owners. Here you will find clear, down-to-earth guidance to help you understand what your company's financial statements are telling you, as well as solid tools to help you run your business more profitably.

The book is written in an easy-to-digest manner that caters to busy entrepreneurs. It contains a blend of instruction and illustrated examples following the story of Joe's Plumbing, a typical small business that is run by Joe and his wife, Becky. Joe's Plumbing

CASE STUDY

Joe runs a local plumbing business along with his wife, Becky. The two of them work hard and are reasonably successful. Joe works from 6 a.m. to 8 p.m. most days and is on call the rest of the time.

If you asked Joe, he would tell you that his major problem is that he gets up, goes to work, comes home, and goes to bed without ever stopping to analyze his business. Am I making money? Am I retaining customers? Am I compensating myself appropriately? The few times he has pondered these questions, he became frustrated and gave up quickly because he did not know how to measure or track his business results.

faces all the problems that most small businesses face: bad record keeping, uncertain cash flow, and a low profit margin.

The information in *Financial Management 101* has been honed from the entrepreneurial seminars, radio broadcasts, and one-to-one training sessions I have done in my accounting firm over the years.

How to use this book

Financial Management 101 walks you through the various aspects of understanding, measuring, and monitoring your financial results. You don't need to read the book in sequence; you can skip around and read it in chunks, absorbing the information that's relevant to you. I do, however, recommend that you eventually read the entire book as it sheds new light on many old subjects. You may find yourself looking at your financial statements differently from now on.

The book provides sound management advice for all small businesses, no matter what country you operate in. The information is not directly related to any particular set of accounting rules or tax laws. Terminology may differ from country to country, and the dollar signs for some readers should be pounds or rupees or lire, but the underlying principles of this book are universally applicable.

Appendix 1 provides a template for your monthly management operating plan. This plan pulls together all the information that we learn to track in this book and gives you a methodology to apply it to your business.

There are many downloadable tools and other useful information at <www.numbers101.com>. Please surf by and download templates, screen savers, and other cool tools — and sign up for our newsletter while you're there.

Financial Management 101 is the second book in the *Numbers 101 for Small Business* series. If you want to brush up on your accounting basics, you may wish to read *Bookkeepers' Boot Camp*, the first book in the series. It covers the essentials of record keeping for small business and why it's necessary to track information. The book also teaches you how to sort through the masses of information and paperwork in your business, how to record what's important for your business, and how to use that information to grow your business for success.

Your business: What is it all about?

How do you look at your business right now? What is it there for? If you are a shoemaker, you might say that the purpose of the business is to provide shoes to customers at a reasonable price. That is your company's positioning strategy.

The underlying purpose of any business is to make money for its stakeholders. Who are the stakeholders? They are the investors in the business. In the case of small business, that's usually the owner/manager, but it could also include outside investors.

The only way for any business to make money is to increase its net profit, cash flow, and return on investment at the same time.

Net profit

Net profit is simply what is left after you have deducted all your company's expenses from its revenues. You can increase your net profit by increasing revenue or decreasing expenses.

Example:

Revenue	**$50,000**
Expenses:	
Cost of goods sold	23,000
Wages	12,500
Rent	9,000
Office supplies	470
	44,970
Net profit	**5,030**

Cash flow

Cash flow represents all the cash that comes into your business less the cash that goes out of your business.

Cash comes in from such sources as —

- cash sales,
- the collection of accounts receivable,
- new borrowings or investment, and
- cash received from the sale of equipment.

Cash goes out of your business to —

- pay your accounts payable,
- make debt repayments,

- purchase new equipment, and
- distribute profits to the owners.

Example:

Cash in:

Cash sales	18,500
Receivables collected	12,500
Proceeds from sale of machine	8,250
	39,250

Cash out:

Payment of payables	23,275
Loan repayments	6,500
Dividends paid to owner	12,500
	42,275
Net cash flow	**(3,025)**

Although the above business is making a positive net profit, the actual money is flowing out faster than it is flowing in. This business would find itself in a cash flow squeeze very quickly.

Return on investment

Return on investment (ROI) is the amount of net profit the business makes, shown as a percentage of how much money the stakeholders have invested in the business. Remember that the stakeholder is usually the owner/manager.

For example, let's assume that when you started your business, you made an initial cash investment of $50,000 and you have not had to invest any further funds in the business. You *could* have taken that $50,000 and put it in an investment certificate yielding 5 percent. If you had done that instead, you would have made $2,500 every year:

$$\$2,500/\$50,000 = 0.05 = 5\%$$

Your return on investment on the investment certificate then would be 5 percent.

However, you didn't invest in the certificate, you invested in your business. So how do we look at the ROI on your business? In exactly the same way. You've invested $50,000. Your business generates $7,550 in net profit annually. Your ROI is:

$$\$7,550/\$50,000 = 0.15 = 15\%$$

Therefore, the same $50,000 would generate an ROI of 15 percent when invested in your business versus 5 percent in an investment certificate. This is a useful way of evaluating your investment in the business and seeing how your investment return changes from year to year. We will discuss investment return in more detail in Chapter 12.

Let's move on to Chapter 1 and take a quick refresher course on the reports that make up your financial statements.

Refresher: Balance Sheet, Income Statement, and Cash Flow Statement

In this chapter, you will learn –

- The basic attributes of the balance sheet, income statement, and cash flow statement
- How the three statements interconnect
- The difference between net income and cash flow

Before we can examine how to interpret your financial information and make valid management decisions based on that information, you need to understand the three basic financial statements of the business and how they work. If, after reading this chapter, you feel that you need to brush up on bookkeeping topics, please refer to *Bookkeepers' Boot Camp,* the first book in the Self-Counsel Press *Numbers 101 for Small Business* series. There you will learn the basics of double-entry bookkeeping and how to prepare your financial statements.

The three basic financial statements for any small business are the —

- balance sheet,
- income statement (sometimes called the profit and loss statement or P&L), and
- cash flow statement (sometimes called the statement of changes in financial position).

We will look at each of these in turn.

The balance sheet

The balance sheet is a freeze-frame picture of the *assets* a business owns and the *liabilities (debts)* a business owes at a particular time. Sample 1 shows a typical balance sheet.

For example, if a business prepared a balance sheet as of December 31, it would show some or all of the following assets:

- Cash in the bank
- Accounts receivable (i.e., amounts to be received from customers)
- Inventory
- Capital assets (e.g., equipment)

And the following liabilities (debts):

- Suppliers that will be paid in the future
- Bank loans and mortgages
- Wages payable to employees

The liabilities are split on the balance sheet between current (those that will be paid within one year) and long term.

The balance sheet also shows the *owner's equity.* This is the sum of —

- retained earnings (i.e., all the historical profits a business has made that have been left in the business),
- capital stock (i.e., the stock that has been purchased by shareholders in a corporation), and
- contributed capital (i.e., any capital funds that have been invested by the owners of the business).

Sample 1
TYPICAL BALANCE SHEET

Balance sheet as at December 31, 200-	
Assets	
Cash	4,250
Accounts receivable	6,975
Inventory	1,200
Capital assets	9,325
Total assets	**21,750**
Liabilities	
Current	
Line of credit payable	3,250
Accounts payable	1,350
Long term	
Equipment loan	8,750
Mortgage on building	2,575
Total liabilities	**15,925**
Equity	
Retained earnings	2,295
Capital stock	100
Contributed capital	3,430
Total equity	**5,825**
Total liabilities and equity	**21,750**

Note that Total assets should equal the Total liabilities and equity

In other words, the owner's equity is the net worth of the business. Another way of valuing net worth is to subtract what the business owes (liabilities) from what the business owns (assets).

Assets - Liabilities = Owner's equity

or

Assets = Liabilities + Owner's equity

One final note to keep in mind about the balance sheet is its valuation. In most countries, accounting rules (called Generally Accepted Accounting Principles or GAAP) require that the balance sheet be valued at historical cost. That means, for example, that if your business bought the building in which it resides in 1982 for $100,000 and it's now worth $295,000, it will still be recorded in the balance sheet at its historical cost of $100,000 (minus depreciation). (For more information on depreciation, consult *Bookkeepers' Boot Camp,* the first book in the Self-Counsel Press *Numbers 101 for Small Business* series.) For this reason, a balance sheet does not always give a business owner the true picture of the value of a business. We will discuss valuation principles in later chapters.

The income statement

The income statement shows the revenue and expense activities of the business for a period of time — be it a day, week, month, or year. See Sample 2 for an example of an income statement.

Sample 2
INCOME STATEMENT

Income statement for XYZ Business for the year ended December 31, 200-	
Revenue	**$50,000**
Expenses	
Cost of goods sold	15,000
Rent	9,570
Wages	6,250
Office supplies	1,290
Total expenses	**32,110**
Net profit	**17,890**

The first section of the income statement shows the business's revenues. This is the amount of sales it has made in the period, regardless of whether or not the money has been collected. For example, if your business sold $50,000 worth of product or services, but you weren't going to collect the money until 90 days after the period end, you would still show the $50,000 as revenue (and you would have $50,000 in Accounts receivable on the balance sheet).

The next section of the income statement shows the business's total expenses for that period, again, regardless of whether or not they have been paid.

The number at the bottom of the income statement is the net profit for the period, calculated by subtracting the total expenses from the revenue.

The cash flow statement

The cash flow statement is the most misunderstood statement in your financial statement package. Its purpose is to show a summary of the sources and uses of a business's cash during a particular period. It answers the critical question, "Where did my cash go?" See Sample 3 for an example of a cash flow statement.

Sample 3
CASH FLOW STATEMENT

Small Company Inc.
Cash flow statement
Year ended 31 December 200-

Net income	$68,812
Add back: Depreciation*	9,340
	78,152
Cash from operating activities	
Increase in Accounts receivable	(5,268)
Increase in Inventory	(4,750)
Decrease in Accounts payable	(26,745)
Increase in Government remittances	463
Increase in Income taxes	77
Increase in Due to shareholder	5,130
Decrease in Mortgage payable	(13,913)
	(45,006)
Cash from investing activities	
Purchase of capital assets	(1,475)
	(1,475)
Cash from financing activities	
Dividends	(40,707)
	(40,707)
Total decrease in cash	(9,036)
Opening cash balance**	10,295
Closing cash balance	$1,259

* For more information on depreciation, read Bookkeepers' Boot Camp.
** The opening cash balance is the ending cash balance from the previous year.

The cash flow statement can take many formats but the most common one breaks the statement into three sections:

- **Cash from operating activities.** This could include the collection of receivables, payment of payables, and purchase of inventory.
- **Cash from investing activities.** This could include the purchase or disposal of equipment.
- **Cash from financing activities.** This could include borrowing new money from lenders, repaying debt to lenders, new capital investments from the owners, and cash distributions to owners.

The sums of all three sections of the cash flow statement plus the net income minus non-cash expences are combined to show the net increase or decrease in cash for the period. For example, if you started your year with $5,000 in the business's bank account and now there was $2,700, the cash flow statement would summarize all the inflows and outflows that make up the net decrease in cash of $2,300.

Chapter summary

➡ The three major financial statements for a business are the balance sheet, income statement, and cash flow statement.

➡ The balance sheet represents a snapshot in time of what a business owns and owes, usually recorded at historical cost.

➡ The income statement represents a business's operating activity for the period leading up to the related balance sheet.

➡ The cash flow statement answers the question, "Where did the money go?" It shows cash inflows and outflows from all activities for the period leading up to the related balance sheet.

Basic Budgeting

In this chapter, you will learn —

- The importance of budgeting
- How to prepare and update a monthly budget report
- What to do with the information

The purpose of this book is to take the basic information that you have about your business's financial position and create a structured plan to maintain, track, and improve your financial performance.

Under half of all businesses that have fewer than five employees maintain a working budget, the most basic of management reports. These businesses give many reasons, including, "I can't predict my sales" and "It takes too much time." However, businesses that have been around for a long time understand the importance of tracking and planning. Without a solid understanding of your impending performance, it is nearly impossible for you to make intelligent financial decisions for your business.

The monthly budget report

The monthly budget report is the most basic of all financial planning tools. It shows what the projected revenues and expenses are for your business for the next one to five years, on a month-by-month basis. The monthly budget report only shows revenues and expenses, not cash receipts and disbursements.

Sample 4 shows a monthly budget report forecasting the next 12 months. The cash flow report is discussed in more detail in Chapter 5.

The monthly budget report in Sample 4 shows some interesting trends. Notice that this business is cyclical (i.e., its revenues flow in cycles). In August, January, and February there are substantial peaks in sales, while in June and October, there is a noticeable dip. This report could be for a retailer who sells lawn and garden equipment and supplies. People start buying in January to get ready for spring and they buy in August to get ready for the fall cleanup. June and October are mid-season where there might not be as much activity.

The monthly budget report is a useful tool for predicting when sales will be high and when they will be low so that you can plan for those events. For example, if your sales are always at a low point in March, it may make sense to target your advertising during that period.

Where do the numbers come from?

In Appendix 1, there is a template that helps you start gathering numbers for your own monthly budget report, which forms part of your monthly management operating plan. If you prefer to work on a spreadsheet, go to <www.numbers101.com> for a free downloadable template.

The starting point for your budget plan is to know what happened in the past. Of course, if you are a start-up business, you won't have any financial history to examine. We will discuss start-ups later in the chapter.

If you work on a computerized accounting program like *MYOB* or *Simply Accounting*, you most likely have historical information at your fingertips. Run your monthly income statement for the previous 12 months. This will give you an overview of your business's financial performance for the past year. You should be able to note the seasonality of your sales and be able to explain the dips and peaks. If you can't explain them, take some time to analyze the sales.

Sample 4
MONTHLY BUDGET REPORT (12 MONTHS)

Small Company Inc.
Monthly budget report
Year ended 29 February, 2005

Account	Mar	Apr	May	Jun	Jul	Aug	Sep	Oct	Nov	Dec	Jan	Feb	Total
Revenue	3,725	4,612	4,109	3,289	5,085	5,139	4,103	3,578	3,945	4,210	6,412	5,303	$53,510
Cost of goods sold	1,895	2,416	1,989	1,675	2,756	2,708	1,965	1,792	2,006	2,165	3,260	2,585	27,212
Advertising	50	50	50	50	50	50	103	50	50	50	50	50	653
Bank charges	7	7	7	7	7	7	7	7	7	7	7	17	94
Office expenses	61	68	66	72	69	65	73	57	53	65	76	71	796
Professional fees	0	0	0	412	0	0	0	0	0	0	0	0	412
Supplies	39	31	42	19	65	58	17	39	42	58	63	51	524
Telephone & utilities	87	89	79	96	85	89	97	89	71	69	59	76	986
Vehicle expenses	39	47	32	45	49	51	34	31	32	41	39	38	478
Wages	306	310	285	296	314	312	342	284	292	325	312	295	3,673
Net income	1,241	1,594	1,559	617	1,690	1,799	1,465	1,229	1,392	1,430	2,546	2,120	18,682

Find out who you sold to during those periods. This knowledge is the foundation of your planning, as knowing why and when customers buy from you helps you to plan the future.

If you do not work on a computerized program, photocopy the template in Appendix 1 and use it to map your monthly performance for the past year.

Revenues

Let's take a look at the revenue side of the monthly budget report first. Okay, so now you know what you did last year. How does it impact what you are going to sell next year? If you're in a stable business, you should be able to expect that you will at least sell the same amount as you did last year. So that's a start. However, it makes sense to always have your sales trending upwards. If you have planned special advertising and promotional events in the upcoming year, you should expect your sales to increase.

If you are a young and rapidly expanding business, look at your rate of growth over the past two or three years. If you are growing at an average of 20 percent per year, for example, budget a 20 percent increase in sales for the upcoming year. To measure your rate of growth from one year to the next, take the difference between the sales figures for both years and divide that difference by the total sales for the first year. For example, if your 2002 sales are $50,000 and your 2003 sales are $67,000, your rate of growth is ($67,000 - $50,000)/50,000 or 34 percent.

Once you have mapped out your revenues, it's time to look at your expenses.

Expenses

Again, looking over your business's monthly income statement for the past year will yield important information about your expenses. You will find certain expenses that never fluctuate, like equipment lease payments and office rent. There will also be expenses that vary, either in step with sales levels or because of other factors. Examples would be office supplies and postage.

Start mapping those expenses that you know for certain. If you are locked into a three-year office lease, you know exactly what your payments will be for the next year. Then start filling in the other expenses. You will need to think about each one as you map it out. For example, if you know that you will be sending out 5,000 flyers in May, make sure that the projected cost is in your advertising budget figure for May. If you are projecting a 20 percent increase in sales, you will probably want to increase your office supply budget.

Your wage cost deserves special attention. It's important to make sure that you are including the full cost of your employees, not just the net checks paid to them. Depending on the regulatory environment in which you operate, you would also have to pay out things for your employee like pension, employment insurance, or health care premiums. These are all costs of having employees and should be included as a projected expense. Also, if you are projecting a big jump in sales, make sure that you can do it with the employees you have. If not, include the wage costs of new employees in your plan.

Chapter summary

➡ Budgeting is a critical process for all businesses that want to last.

➡ Review your monthly performance from last year and make sure that you can tell the story of the numbers.

➡ Make sure your budget numbers are consistent with your operating strategy.

➡ Review your 12-month budget every month, dropping off the old month and adding one on at the end.

Chapter

3

Variable versus Fixed Costs: Why You Need to Know the Difference

In this chapter, you will learn —

- How to classify your business's expenses into fixed or variable expenses

- How costs behave when your production volume changes

- Why "losing money on every unit but making it up on volume" doesn't work

- How to determine your business's capacity

Let's take a look at cost behavior, that is, finding out how particular costs are affected by events such as changing sales levels, increases or decreases in other costs, and the purchase of new assets.

At first glance, it may appear that this kind of analysis of your financials is time consuming and boring, but all successful and long-lasting businesses understand cost behavior. This will help you better understand the mechanics of your business and will allow you to plan for growth with confidence.

CASE STUDY

Fixed versus variable expenses

Your business's expenses can all be categorized by their behavior, that is, by whether or not they vary with the level of your business's revenues. The expenses on your income statement are either fixed or variable.

Variable expenses

These expenses vary directly with the sales revenue of the business. The most common examples of variable costs are cost of goods sold (in the case of a retailer) and cost of goods produced (in the case of a manufacturer).

Let's say you sell a product for $10 a unit and your cost to purchase that unit is $8. Your variable cost is $8 a unit. (The cost is variable because it depends on how many products you sell.) Therefore, if you have $1,000 in sales, your cost of goods sold is $800. If you have $100,000 in sales, your cost is $80,000. The cost of goods sold will always vary in a direct relationship with sales volume.

The only way to change variable costs is to do one of the following:

- Renegotiate your purchase contracts with your goods or materials suppliers
- Purchase cheaper product (although, that may very well have an impact on how much you can sell the product for)
- Purchase in greater volume to get higher purchase discounts (although, you may also have a higher cost of warehousing your inventory)

Fixed expenses

These are expenses that are independent of the sales volume. This means that even if you do not sell $1 worth of your product or service, you will still incur these costs.

Rent, utilities, and office wages are some examples of fixed expenses. Whether or not you are selling anything, you still need a place to run your business, to have lights on, and to pay someone to answer the telephones.

It's important to note that fixed expenses are only fixed in the short run. Eventually, when your sales volumes increase, you will need a larger warehouse, more power for the equipment, and more office staff. However, for the time being, we will only look at the range of sales volume in which the fixed expenses remain constant.

Why is cost behavior important to my business?

So, why do you need to know how your costs behave? Because, armed with that information, you can analyze your income statement and plan for business growth. Two critical concepts fall out of cost behavior analysis: break-even point and capacity.

Break-even point

Your business's break-even point is the point where your revenues are sufficient to cover your expenses. Remember, even if you don't sell anything, you still have fixed costs to cover.

Consider the following example:

Revenue per unit	$10
Cost per unit	7
Gross margin	3

So, for every unit you sell, you net $3. Now, what if your fixed expenses looked like this:

Rent	$7,500
Utilities	1,250
Wages	9,470
Office supplies	595
Total fixed expenses	18,815

How many units would you have to sell to cover your fixed expenses?

$$\$18,815/\$3 = 6,272 \text{ units}$$

You would need to sell 6,272 units to keep the doors open. If you sell more, you make a profit. If you sell fewer, you will lose money.

Instead of looking at the number of units you need to sell to break even, you can also calculate the total sales you need to make. Using the above example, we would start by calculating a gross margin percentage (GM%).

$$GM\% = GM \text{ per unit/Revenue per unit} = \$3/\$10 = 30\%$$

Break-even sales would then be —

$$Overhead/GM\% = \$18,815/0.30 = \$62,717$$

You would therefore need to have revenues of $62,717 to be able to keep the doors open.

Most small businesses never take the time to calculate their break-even point. Most feel that their revenues will be whatever they are and that they can't do anything about them. You can see from the above example why it would be important to know how much your sales have to be in order to survive.

Capacity

Not only is it important to know how much you need to sell in order to keep the doors open, you need to know how much you can do in sales with your current fixed cost structure. This is called capacity. If you're a manufacturer, your plant and equipment will only physically handle so many units before you need to move to a larger premises and purchase new equipment. If you're in a service business, as your revenue levels start to increase, you will need to hire more staff and have larger offices.

Think of the break-even point as the minimum you need to do and capacity as the most you can do.

For example, let's look at a business that manufactures dolls. The business has a combined plant/warehouse and employs 35 manufacturing staff. The owner has analyzed the equipment, space, and staff, and has determined the following:

Maximum units manufacturing equipment can produce	12,500
Maximum units warehouse can store	10,475
Maximum production of manufacturing staff	14,675

This analysis tells us that the warehouse space is the limiting factor, or the bottleneck, in the business. No matter how hard the staff work or how hard the equipment is run, the warehouse can only handle 10,475 units. This is the capacity of the current cost structure.

Why is this important information? If the owner is budgeting and forecasting for the upcoming year and budgets any more than 10,475 units to be produced, she must also plan for more space — which increases her fixed costs. She would then have to determine whether the profit from the additional units offsets the new cost of larger warehousing space.

This concept is also valid for service businesses. Let's assume your business provides consulting services. You are the owner and chief consultant and you have two other consultants working with you.

You want to calculate your capacity. Look at the following figures:

Number of hours in a work year (per person)	1,950
Average number of hours spent on admin. activities	250
Number of hours available to charge to clients	1,700
Average charge-out rate	$75

Each of the three consultants should be able to charge out 1,700 times $75 annually to clients. This is then multiplied by the number of consultants:

$$1,700 \times \$75 \times 3 = \$382,500$$

This means that the maximum revenue with your current cost structure is $382,500. It would be ridiculous to budget for revenue of $500,000 without planning for a new staff member.

CASE STUDY

"So, based on my calculations," Becky said, " we would need to make sure that the new employee has at least 20 hours of billable work a week in order to pay for his salary."

"That's right," said Vivian. "And you were telling me that, with your expected increase in commercial construction work, you should easily be able to get the 20 hours. So it makes sense to hire an employee."

"I'll get the ad in the paper today," said Becky.

Chapter summary

➡ Fixed costs are costs that do not change with volume of sales.

➡ Variable costs are costs that do change with changes to the sales volumes.

➡ The break-even calculation tells you how much of your product or service you have to sell in order to cover your fixed costs.

➡ The capacity calculation tells you the maximum number of units of your product or service you can produce or provide with your current operating facilities.

Chapter
4

Ratio Analysis for Fun and Profit

In this chapter, you will learn —

- Why ratio analysis is critical to successful businesses

- The basic ratios and what they tell you

- How to pick the ratios that best foretell your business's success

- What to do when ratios indicate a problem

- How to integrate ratios into your management reporting system

The subject of ratios is one that makes most small business owners' heads hurt. Financial analysts and stockbrokers regularly assess the ratios of large, publicly traded companies, but many small businesses do not even consider ratios when they prepare their financial information. Why should you care about ratios? Consider the following reasons:

- Your bank will certainly care about monitoring ratios. They want to see how you're doing in comparison with other businesses that they are lending to, and in comparison to the standards they have set for lending.

- Ratios are excellent indicators of financial health. Much like a high blood pressure or cholesterol reading at your doctor's office would signal impending physical trouble, out-of-kilter ratios signal financial trouble for your business.

- Ratios are a useful tool for comparing your business activities year over year. For example, is your working capital ratio steadily improving or not? (We will discuss this and other ratios later in the chapter.)

- Ratios are a useful tool for comparing your business activities with those of other businesses. Without using ratios, it can be difficult to compare businesses of different sizes.

The basic ratios and what they tell you

Ratios can be grouped into different categories based on the type of information they provide:

- Solvency or liquidity ratios (e.g., current ratio, total debt ratio)

- Asset and debt management ratios (e.g., inventory turnover, times interest earned, payables turnover, receivables turnover)

- Profitability ratios (e.g., profit margin, return on assets, return on investment)

Check out Table 1 at the end of the chapter for a summary of all the ratios we'll discuss.

Solvency or liquidity ratios

Solvency ratios (sometimes called liquidity ratios) indicate how well your business can pay its bills in the short term without straining cash flows. As you can well imagine, your lenders are usually quite interested in the short-term solvency of your business. (They want to make sure they get their money back!) Some commonly calculated solvency ratios are:

- Current ratio

- Total debt ratio

Current ratio

The current ratio is one of the best measures of whether you have enough resources to pay your bills in the next twelve months. It is calculated as —

Current ratio = Current assets/Current liabilities

The current ratio can be expressed in either dollar figures or times covered. For example, a business has total current assets of $4,325 and current liabilities of $3,912. The business's current ratio would be —

Current ratio = Current assets/Current liabilities

= $4,325/$3,912 = 1.11 : 1

In other words, for every dollar in current liabilities, there is $1.11 in current assets. You could also say that the business has its current liabilities covered 1.11 times over. For a refresher on current assets and current liabilities, refer to *Bookkeepers' Boot Camp*, the first book in the *Numbers 101 for Small Business* series.

To a lender, the higher the ratio, the more secure is their investment in your business. The same is generally true for you as the business manager; you want the ratio to be at least one or greater. However, if your current ratio is higher than normal for your business, it may indicate that you are not using your resources effectively. This might happen because you have one (or all) of the following situations:

- Abnormally high inventory levels (i.e., you are over stocking the pantry)
- Surplus cash sitting in the bank that should be invested long term (or used to pay down current liabilities)
- An accounts receivable collection problem

Total debt ratio

The total debt ratio measures the long-term solvency of your business. It shows you how highly your business is leveraged, or in debt. The total debt ratio is calculated as:

Total debt ratio = Total debt/Total assets

Just like the current ratio, you can express the total debt ratio in dollars or times. For example, if a business has a total debt of $12,673 and total assets of $9,412, its total debt ratio would be —

Total debt ratio = Total debt/Total assets

= $12,673/$9,412 = 1.35 : 1

In other words, for every dollar you have in assets, the business has $1.35 in liabilities. You could also say that the business is leveraged 135 percent or that its assets cover its liabilities 0.74 times over ($9,412/$12,673).

In the case of the total debt ratio, you would want the result to be one or less. The lower the ratio, the less total debt the business has in comparison with its asset base.

The total debt ratio would be of interest to your long-term lenders. For example, if your business owned the plant in which it operates and the bank has loaned the business money by way of mortgage against the property, the bank would be very interested in the long-term health of your business. Highly leveraged businesses risk becoming insolvent and declaring bankruptcy.

Asset and debt management ratios

Asset and debt management ratios tell you how well your business is managing its resources to generate sales. There are four main ratios in this category:

- Inventory turnover
- Receivables turnover
- Payables turnover
- Times interest earned

Inventory turnover

The inventory turnover ratio answers the question, "How long does my inventory sit before it gets sold?" This is an important question because there are warehousing and other costs associated with holding inventory. The ratio is calculated as follows:

Inventory turnover = Cost of goods sold/Ending inventory

If a business's cost of goods sold (COGS) during a period is $87,621 and its cost of goods remaining in inventory at the end of the period is $9,783, the inventory turnover ratio would be —

Inventory turnover = $87,621/$9,783 = 9.0 times

We could say that we can turn over our inventory nine times in a year. A more useful interpretation is to calculate days' sales in inventory, which is —

365 days/Inventory turnover = 365/9.0 = 40.6 days

This tells us that, on average, the inventory sits for almost 41 days before it is sold. Some businesses use the average inventory for the year (beginning inventory plus ending inventory divided by two) and some businesses use the ending inventory for this calculation. It all depends on what you want to track. Using average inventory gives you a historical perspective (i.e., what happened during the year), whereas using the ending inventory gives you a forward look at your current inventory levels.

In general, you would want this ratio to be as low as possible without having chronic shortages of inventory on hand. In a perfect world, inventory would materialize at exactly the time it's needed for a sale. The inventory turnover ratio tells you how long you generally hold the inventory before it's sold.

Receivables turnover

While the inventory turnover ratio tells you how quickly you can sell your goods, the receivables turnover ratio tells you how quickly you generally get the money for the sale into your bank account. The receivables turnover ratio is calculated much like the inventory turnover ratio:

Receivables turnover = Sales/Accounts receivable

If your sales were $113,423 and your receivables balance was $18,903, the ratio would be calculated as —

Receivables turnover = $113,423/$18,903 = 6.0 times

We can also look at the average number of days before collection:

Days' sales in receivables = 365 days/Receivables turnover

= 365/6.0 = 60.8 days

This tells us that, on average, we collect our receivables in just over 60 days. If our credit terms are net 30, this indicates a problem. We would need to examine our credit and collection policies to find out why we don't get our money in 30 days.

Payables turnover

Payables turnover is the flip side of the receivables turnover. It tells us how quickly we pay our suppliers. It is calculated as:

Payables turnover = COGS/Accounts payable

If our cost of goods sold is $87,621 and our payables are $16,411, the payables turnover ratio would be calculated as —

Payables turnover = COGS/Accounts payable

$87,621/$16,411 = 5.3 times

The average number of days before we pay our suppliers is —

= 365 days/Payables turnover

= 365 days/5.3 = 68.9 days

This tells us that, on average, we pay our suppliers in almost 69 days. If our suppliers' terms are net 30, we are probably incurring late payment penalties and interest. This isn't the most efficient use of our resources. On the other hand, if our suppliers' terms are net 30 and we pay on average in 15 days, we are prepaying our liabilities, which also is not a good use of our resources.

Times interest earned

The times interest earned calculation tells us how able we are to meet the interest obligations to our creditors. It is calculated as follows:

Times interest earned = Earnings before interest and taxes (EBIT)/Interest expense

If our earnings before interest and taxes (EBIT) is $23,496 and our interest expense is $2,674, then the ratio is —

Times interest earned = $23,496/$2,674 = 8.8 times

This means we could have paid our interest expense almost nine times over. In general, the higher the ratio, the "safer" the business is. It is critical to note, though, that this ratio only looks at the interest portion of our creditor obligations, not the required principal repayments. The principal repayments are part of the current ratio (for principal repayments due in the next 12 months) and the total debt ratio (for all principal repayments).

Profitability ratios

The last major category of ratios is profitability ratios. These measure how effectively you are able to use your resources to produce profit. We will look at three ratios in this category:

- Profit margin
- Return on assets
- Return on investment

Profit margin

The profit margin is a common measure of how well you can translate gross sales into bottom-line profit. It is calculated as —

Profit margin = Net income/Sales

If your sales are $113,423 and your net income is $22,475, your profit margin is —

Profit margin = Net income/Sales
= $22,475/$113,423 = 19.8%

This tells you that for every dollar of sales, you are generating almost 20 cents in net profit. As you can well imagine, in general, the higher the profit margin, the better off the business.

Return on assets (ROA)

Your assets are what allow you to generate profit, and the return on assets ratio (ROA) shows you how effectively you are using your assets to generate profit. It is calculated as:

ROA = Net income/Total assets

If your net income is $22,475 and your total assets are $73,810, the ROA would be —

ROA = Net income/Total assets

= $22,475/$73,810 = 30%

You can also say that for every dollar of assets you have on the balance sheet, you generate 30 cents of net profit. The higher the ratio, generally, the more effective you are at using your assets to generate profit.

Return on investment (ROI)

Return on investment (ROI) is one of the least calculated and most important ratios for small businesses. It tells you what kind of return you are getting from the personal money that you have invested in your business.

For example, let's say that when you started up the business, you took $7,500 from your savings account and used that money for start-up expenses. You could have taken that same money and invested it in a bond (where it would earn interest income) or in real estate (where it would earn rental income) or in one of many other investments. But you chose instead to invest in your own small business. Shouldn't you be making a return on that investment? Absolutely!

In Chapter 12 we delve deeper into the issue of return on investment. For now, here's how we calculate it:

ROI = Normalized net income/Money invested

What do we mean by "normalized" net income? We want to calculate net income as if you are being properly compensated for the hours you work in the business. This is your "employee" or "manager" role. How do you know what you're worth? Start by calculating how much you would have to pay someone else to step into your shoes as the manager of the business. For example, if you would have to hire a replacement for $47,000 and you are only paying yourself $25,000 in order to take it easy on cash flow, then you would subtract the difference ($22,000) from income to get to normalized net income.

$$\text{ROI} = \text{Normalized net income/Money invested}$$
$$= (\$22{,}475 - \$22{,}000)/\$7{,}500 = 6.3\%$$

This means that you are making a 6.3 percent return on your investment in the business. This is probably better than a savings account but not enough to compensate you for the risk of investing in a small business. On top of that, you're getting paid $25,000 for a $47,000 job. You have a ball and chain around your ankle because you can never leave your business. You would have a difficult time finding someone to take over your business and make that kind of money. It is not a very cheery outlook!

Which ratios should my business track?

Whew! That's a lot of numbers! You are probably wondering if you need to track them all on an ongoing basis. Of course not. Some ratios will be more applicable to certain businesses and certain industries than others. For example, if you provide a service instead of a product, the inventory turnover and return on assets may not be relevant to you, but the receivables turnover may be critical to the efficient operation of your business.

Choose the most important four or five ratios for your business and track those as part of your monthly management operating plan. Appendix 1 contains a space to write down your chosen ratios for future reference.

When good ratios go bad: What to do when there's a problem

Okay, so you have chosen the important ratios you want your business to track and you are tracking them on a quarterly basis. In the third quarter, three of the ratios seem out of kilter. What do you do? How do you know what's going wrong?

Here is a quick guide to the questions you need to ask yourself and your team if your ratios seem to be deteriorating.

Solvency or liquidity ratios:

- Do I have too much debt?
- Are my debt repayment terms too hard on cash flow?
- Am I getting behind on my payments to my suppliers?

Asset and debt management ratios:

- Am I buying too much inventory?
- Am I collecting my receivables on time?
- Can I stretch out my payables without causing harm to my supplier relationships?

Profitability ratios

- Are my expenses under control?
- Do I have a lot of excess cash in my account?
- Have my sales dropped and why?

After three or four quarters of tracking your ratios, you will have a much better understanding of your business: its cycles, its cash flow patterns, and its idiosyncrasies. Only once you understand your business on this level can you really start to grow!

Chapter summary

➡ Solvency ratios measure your business's ability to meet its debt obligations.

➡ Asset and debt management ratios measure how your business manages its resources to generate sales.

➡ Profitability ratios measure how effectively you are able to use those resources to produce profit.

➡ Ratios are most useful when compared over time.

Table 1
A QUICK REFERENCE TO RATIOS

Solvency or liquidity ratios

    1. Current ratio = Current assets/Current liabilities

    Am I going to be able to pay my short-term debts?

    2. Total debt ratio = Total debt/Total assets

    How much leverage do I have?

Asset and debt management ratios

    3. Inventory turnover = COGS/Inventory

    How long before I sell my product?

    4. Receivables turnover = Sales/Accounts receivable

    How long before I get paid for what I sell?

    5. Payables turnover = COGS/Accounts payable

    How quickly do I pay my suppliers?

    6. Times interest earned = EBIT/Interest expense

    Do I have enough income to pay the interest on my debt?

Profitability ratios

    7. Profit margin = Net income/Sales

    How efficiently am I managing my expenses?

    8. Return on assets = Net profit/Total assets

    How well am I using my assets to generate profit?

    **9. Return on investment =
Normalized net income/money invested**

    What kind of return am I getting on the money I've put into the business?

Understanding the Operating Cycle

In this chapter, you will learn —

- How to use your ratio information
- What the operating cycle is and how to understand yours
- The difference between short- and long-term cycles
- How to manage the operating cycles to improve cash flow

In the previous chapters, we've discussed your financial statements and the relationship between the numbers. You are now familiar with some of your key ratios and can interpret what they mean.

In this chapter, we're going to look at the operating cycles of your business — from the ordering of inventory through to payment by the customer, from the money coming in from a new loan through to the repayment process.

Understanding the ebbs and flows of cash in your business is critical to scouting for warning signs of impending cash crunches. It's one thing to know that you will be getting money in the door, but without knowing when, you're going to be left not knowing if you can pay the bills.

The operating cycle

The activities that your business carries out can be broken down into several events. For a manufacturing business, these main events would be —

1. Buying the raw materials
2. Paying for the raw materials
3. Manufacturing the product
4. Selling the product
5. Collecting cash from the customer

For a retail business, the events are similar:

1. Buying the product to resell
2. Paying for the product
3. Selling the product
4. Collecting cash from the customer

And for a service business, the events would be —

1. Selling the service to the client
2. Performing the service
3. Collecting cash from the customer

As you can see, the basic operations of all types of businesses are similar. These events form a cycle of the conversion of cash back into cash. The operating cycle has two halves: the purchase cycle (the conversion of cash to inventory to cost of goods sold) and the sales cycle (the conversion of cost of goods sold to accounts receivable and back into cash). See Diagram 1 for an illustration of the operating cycle.

Diagram 1
THE OPERATING CYCLE

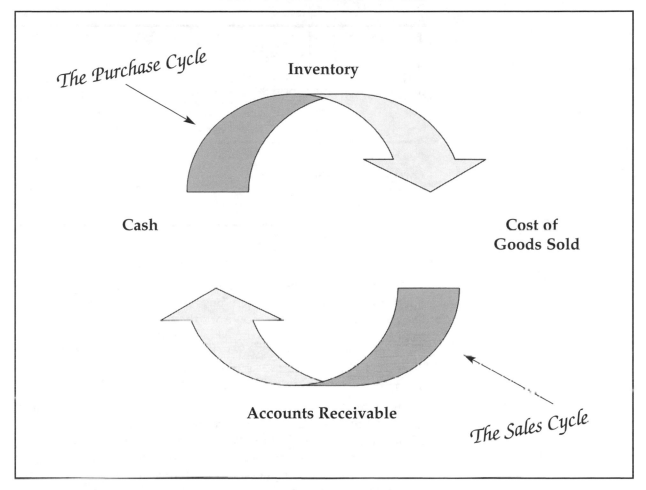

We will use a retail business in our examples for this chapter, but the principles apply to all types of businesses. Let's have a look at a simple example:

One day, you purchase inventory for your store for $100. You pay the bill to the supplier 30 days later. After 15 more days, a customer buys the product for $125. Your customer buys on credit so she does not actually pay you for another 45 days. Here's what it looks like in a timeline:

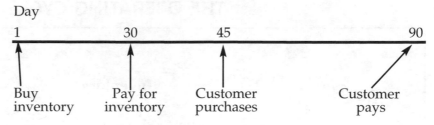

The operating cycle timeline

Day

1   30   45   90

Buy inventory   Pay for inventory   Customer purchases   Customer pays

45 days

Inventory holding period

60 days

Cash float

Many small businesses only look at the fact that they are selling the inventory for more than they are buying it. They know that they are making a profit. However, they miss the fact that it is a total (in this example) of 45 days between the inventory coming in the door and going out the door (known as the inventory holding period), and it is a 60-day span between cash going out the door and cash coming in (the cash float).

So, why do we need to know the inventory holding period and the cash float? Because we need to make sure that we can pay for the inventory when it's due. We know that we can't rely on selling the inventory and getting paid first. There's a 60-day cash flow gap between us paying suppliers and customers paying us. How are we going to finance it?

The cash flow report

Now that we have some basic information on the flow of our cash in the business, we need to integrate that information into a comprehensive plan so that we will be able to predict times when we will be short on cash and times when we will have extra cash that we can invest.

One way to do that is to prepare a monthly cash flow report and to update it frequently as new information becomes available.

The cash flow report looks much like the monthly budget report we created in Chapter 2, with a few notable exceptions:

Monthly budget report	Cash flow report
• shows revenues and expenses	• shows cash in and cash out
• uses the accrual method	• uses the cash method
• puts items in the month occurring	• puts items in the month cash moves

For example, in the cash flow report we don't care how much we are going to have in revenue this month. We only care about how much we're going to collect from customers for revenues generated this month and all prior months.

Revenues

Let's just look at the revenue side for a moment. Let's assume our monthly budget report showed us this information:

	Jan	Feb	Mar	Apr	May
Revenue	$1,250	1,095	2,470	1,750	975

So we know that we should be able to bill those amounts. But what do we know about when we're going to get the money? We already know our average receivable turnaround time (this is the receivables turnover, calculated in the previous chapter). If we receive the money in 37 days on average, is that enough information? Not quite.

It's good to know the average but it's important to know the percentage of revenue we will receive in each month. We can do that by looking at our historical cash receipts and seeing what the patterns look like.

Let's assume we know the following: We will probably collect 15 percent of the March billings in March. This means that 85 percent of all of our March revenues will be collected in the future. We know that we'll probably get 63 percent of the revenues in April. This makes sense considering that, on average, we collect in 37 days. We have now collected 78 percent of all our March billings. A further 18 percent will be collected in May, and, assuming that we have no bad debts, the rest (4 percent) will be collected in June.

Therefore, in June, we will be collecting 4 percent of March's billings, 18 percent of April's billings, 63 percent of May's billings, and 15 percent of June's billings. We have now determined our expected cash inflows. They will look like this:

	Jan	Feb	Mar	Apr	May
Revenue	1,250.00	1,095.00	2,470.00	1,750.00	975.00
Collected:					
Current (15%)	187.50	164.25	370.50	262.50	146.25
Next month (63%)		787.50	689.85	1,556.10	1,102.50
2 months (18%)			225.00	197.10	444.60
3 months (4%)				50.00	43.80
Totals				**2,065.70**	**1,737.15**

Of course, this is only a snapshot. There would also be collections in January to March of prior periods. In our example where we are collecting money every month from four different periods, there would be four lines in every month.

So, in May, even though we are billing $975, we are expecting to collect $1,737.15. We can also predict that June will have a significant bite taken out of its cash flow. Even though we may bill a large amount in June, we didn't in May, and we are collecting 63 percent of May's billings in June. This information is very useful to us as we now know what we expect to be in our bank account in any given month.

Expenses

The expense side of the cash flow report is similar to the revenue side. We want to put expenses into the periods we expect to pay them, not the period in which they belong. So, for example, if we buy new stationery from our printer for $1,000 in May, but we don't pay him until June, that expense would be in May on the monthly budget report but in June on the cash flow report.

Bringing it all together

In Appendix 1, there is a blank template for you to fill out as part of your monthly management operating plan. You can also download a free spreadsheet template at <www.numbers101.com>.

Sample 5 shows a typical cash flow report. Notice that there is a cumulative cash balance on the bottom line. This is how much money should actually be in your bank account by the end of that month. It is critical to monitor this figure. If your cumulative cash is negative at any point, it means that you have run out of money. You will need to make sure that you have a plan in place to temporarily finance these types of shortfalls.

Sample 5
CASH FLOW REPORT

Small Company Inc.
Cash flow report
January – December 2004

	Jan	Feb	Mar	Apr	May	Jun	Jul	Aug	Sep	Oct	Nov	Dec	Total
Cash receipts	3,725	4,612	4,109	3,289	5,085	5,139	4,103	3,578	3,945	4,210	6,412	5,303	53,510
Cost of goods sold	1,895	2,416	1,989	1,675	2,756	2,708	1,965	1,792	2,006	2,165	3,260	2,585	27,212
Advertising	50	50	50	50	50	50	103	50	50	50	50	50	653
Bank charges	7	7	7	7	7	7	7	7	7	7	7	17	94
Office expenses	61	68	66	72	69	65	73	57	53	65	76	71	796
Professional fees	-	-	-	412	-	-	-	-	-	-	-	-	412
Supplies	39	31	42	19	65	58	17	39	42	58	63	51	524
Telephone and utilities	87	89	79	96	85	89	97	89	71	69	59	76	986
Vehicle expenses	39	47	32	45	49	51	34	31	32	41	39	38	478
Wages	306	310	285	296	314	312	342	284	292	325	312	295	3,673
Purchase of capital equipment	-	-	-	1,953	-	475	-	-	-	710	-	-	3,138
Net cash inflow (outflow)	1,241	1,594	1,559	(1,336)	1,690	1,324	1,465	1,229	1,392	720	2,546	2,120	15,544
Opening cash	1,259	2,500	4,094	5,653	4,317	6,007	7,331	8,796	10,025	11,417	12,137	14,683	
Closing cash	2,500	4,094	5,653	4,317	6,007	7,331	8,796	10,025	11,417	12,137	14,683	16,803	

"This is exactly what I was talking about," Joe said, pointing at the computer screen. In the spring and fall months when we're busiest, the cash flow is negative. That's why it always feels like we have no money. What's going on?"

"It's actually quite simple once we look at this cash flow projection in relation to the ratio analysis we've done so far." Vivian swiveled her chair to let both Becky and Joe see the computer. "When you do plumbing repair and installation, you have to buy the parts up front in order to do the work. You always pay your supplier within 30 days. However, as we determined with our ratio analysis, your average receivable takes 53 days to collect. Therefore, you've had to put out the money for the parts 23 days before you get money from the customer. You can see why this problem gets amplified the busier you get."

Becky thought for a moment. "So it doesn't even help when we buy parts only as needed. We're still financing them for almost a month."

"That's right," said Vivian. "We have to start working on your sales billing and collection policies and procedures, and decrease that 53 days."

Chapter summary

➡ The operating cycle of a business represents the time it takes a business to convert cash back into cash.

➡ It's critical to understand the operating timeline so that you can accurately plan cash inflows and outflows.

➡ The cash flow report tracks the projected cash inflows and outflows related to a business's operations.

➡ The cash flow report helps you predict when you will need outside sources of financing for cash shortfalls.

Key Performance Indicators: Your Keys to Success

In this chapter, you will learn —

- Why your business needs to discover its critical success factors
- Why key performance indicators can tell you if you're on the right track
- How to design your own key performance indicator management system
- What to do when your key performance indicators slide

What is the purpose of your business? What do you absolutely need to do in order for your business to succeed? What are the activities that you cannot get wrong without losing significant amounts of business?

These questions are answered by examining your critical success factors (CSFs). Critical success factors are defined as those activities that a business undertakes that allow it to succeed.

They are more than just the numbers on your financial statements. Some CSFs relate to measures of quality, customer satisfaction, and how efficiently you are using your resources.

How do I figure out what my CSFs are?

Now that you know what CSFs are, you need to define the ones that are most important to your business. Take a few moments to answer the following questions:

1. My business is better than my competitors because:
   _____

2. My customers always say that they like it when:
   _____

3. My customers always say that they don't like it when:
   _____

4. If I stopped _____, my customers would start going elsewhere.

Note that two of the four questions relate to your customers' perception of your business, not your impressions of what they think. It's an important distinction because your customers may have a very different view of you and your business than you do. How do you know what your customers think? Ask them! Set up a procedure where they are asked to fill out a feedback form when they purchase your product or service. Ask them what they like and don't like. Ask why they might choose to shop elsewhere. Ask what you are doing well and what you could be doing better. You may be surprised by the results.

The answers to the four questions above give you a list of those activities that you need to make sure your business is doing regularly and consistently. These are your critical success factors. Review your list. You will most likely find that the items on it relate more to your customers' perceived value in your product or service, not just the cost. Businesses that compete only on cost will always suffer in the long run because there will always be someone else that can do the same job for cheaper.

How can I measure my CSFs?

Now that you have defined your critical success factors, you need to be able to make sure you are on track. But how to measure them, especially when some are non-financial?

The measurements of critical success factors are called key performance indicators (KPIs). If critical success factors are things your business must do to thrive, then key performance indicators are the measures of those things.

Here is a typical list of critical success factors:

1. **Personal service:** Making sure the customer gets to speak with a staff member when the purchase is made.

2. **Product quality:** Making sure the product does what you say it will do and is durable.

3. **Quick problem resolution:** Making sure all customer complaints are handled quickly and in a manner that impresses the customer.

4. **Same-day shipping:** Making sure that your product gets shipped out to your customer the day the order is received.

All four of these CSFs can be measured, even though some of them are non-financial. Some examples of the key performance indicators that would track whether you are on-target with your CSFs are:

1. **Personal service:** Provide every customer with a feedback form when he or she purchases your product or service. One of the questions should be, "Was a staff member available to answer all your questions?" Your KPI then becomes how many times "No" is reported on the surveys.

2. **Product quality:** Track how many returns and exchanges customers make. Have a target number. Any number above that is unacceptable.

3. **Quick problem resolution:** Have staff members fill out a standard form when customer complaints occur, outlining both the problem and its resolution.

   Have a staff member follow up with a telephone call to the customer seven days after the incident to ask if the customer is happy with the resolution. The measures could be the satisfaction rating of the customer and the number of days between the initial complaint and the customer's satisfaction.

4. **Same-day shipping:** Track the number of times the product was not shipped same-day.

Those are some of the ways that non-financial indicators can be measured and tracked. Once the measures have been determined, it's important to set your expectations to measure against. For example, if your target is to ship 100 percent of your products same-day, then you would gauge the actual against the standard (100 percent).

In Appendix 1 there is a worksheet for you to fill out your business's CSFs and KPIs. These will become part of your monthly management operating plan.

What happens when my key performance indicators start to slide?

You've been tracking your key performance indicators for months and this month, several of the indicators seem to show problems. What do you do?

When this happens (as it inevitably will), you need to discover the source of the problem. A business could face many problems that would impact its key performance indicators, including employee illness, cash flow crunch, breakdown in processes, and inattentiveness to customer needs. If the problem is short term, such as employee illness, there is no need to take drastic action. However, you will want to see if there is a way to make your operations less vulnerable to the illness of a single employee.

If the problem seems to be in the underlying processes, it's time to put new procedures in place to make sure the critical success factor is being met. Have there been changes in the external business environment? New competitors in the industry? Quality control problems with the inventory? These are all situations that need a rethinking and reformulation of your business plan. If you can see the icebergs, you will have a much better chance of being able to steer around them.

Chapter summary

➡ Solicit regular feedback from your customers on what you're doing right, what you need to improve upon, and what new things your customers would like to see you do.

➡ Critical success factors (CSFs) are those things that your business must get right in order to succeed.

➡ Key performance indicators (KPIs) are the tools with which to measure your critical success factors. They may be either financial or non-financial measures.

➡ Continual measuring of your actual performance to your expected performance will help you determine whether you need to make changes in your business strategy.

Chapter
7

Getting a Grip on Your Inventory

In this chapter, you will learn —

- The true cost of carrying inventory

- The different types of inventory

- How to track your inventory

- How to set up an inventory management system

Inventory is frequently a business's most significant investment. For a retailer, it sometimes reaches over 25 percent of the total assets of the business. Because inventory represents a part of the operating cycle, it's important for businesses of all sizes to manage it prudently and to shorten the period where a business's cash is tied up in inventory.

Inventory management is not taught in most basic business start-up books. In large businesses, it is a specialty unto itself, handled by inventory management or purchasing specialists. In a small business, however, the owner is most likely performing most, if not all, functions, including this critical one.

We will look first at types of inventory and what is included in the cost of those inventories. Then we'll look at inventory management techniques to help you move your inventory more efficiently.

Types of inventory

The type of inventory you carry depends on the type of business you have. Retailers, manufacturers, and service industries look at inventories in different ways.

Retailers

Inventory is straightforward for retailers. It is the costs of what the business buys in order to resell. For example, if your business sells hats, your inventory is the hats that you have purchased to resell but that haven't yet been sold. The inventory in a retail environment constitutes a large portion of the business's assets. Retailers must maintain display space for the products, as well as storage space for excess product. You can't simply stack your products up to the rafters and expect people to come in and dig through the piles. This is especially true of businesses that sell retail to individual customers (as opposed to businesses).

Manufacturers

Inventory in a manufacturing environment is a little more complicated than for retailers. Manufacturers take several different raw materials and apply machining and labor to them to produce a finished product. There are three main types of inventory for manufacturers: raw materials, goods-in-process, and finished goods.

Raw materials are the inputs to the process. They are the goods that the manufacturer has to buy to use in the manufacturing process. For example, if a business makes dining-room furniture, the raw materials would be lumber, nails, screws, and any hardware that is attached during the process. In some cases, the raw materials coming in have already had some processing done to them by the seller. An example of this would be a business that puts together computers. They would need to purchase motherboards and hard drives, which have already been assembled by the vendor.

Goods-in-process are those items on which work has been started, but not completed. Using the example from above of the dining-room furniture, goods-in-process would include table legs and table tops that have been shaped but not yet assembled. The larger and more complex the products manufactured, the longer the finishing time and the larger percentage of inventory will be in this category.

Finished goods are those products that have worked their way through the manufacturing process and are completed but not yet sold or shipped. Finished goods usually take up the most space to store until sale, so it is critical for a manufacturer to manage its finished goods inventory.

Service business

We don't usually think about a business that provides services as having inventory. However, for businesses like lawyers, accountants, and architects, management of inventory is just as important as for businesses that produce goods. Any service business that puts in time to customer projects before payment carries an inventory of time.

Let's look at an example. An architect is hired to produce sketches and then a final blueprint for a shopping mall. Three staff at the business are working on the project. Many activities have to happen to complete the project, including:

- Photographing the site
- Reviewing the client's specifications
- Drawing preliminary sketches
- Holding meetings with the other members of the business
- Presenting sketches to the client
- Revising the sketches and re-presenting
- Drafting the final blueprint
- Overseeing construction

In all likelihood, the invoice will not be presented to the client until they have approved the final blueprint. When they do invoice the client, it will be for the hours put into the project. These hours represent the business's inventory until they are billed out.

It is important to manage this time inventory for several reasons.

- You need to make sure that the time inventory for a particular client is in line with the budgeted project time. For example, if you've quoted a client $1,000 for a job and you have a time inventory of $2,000, you will be unlikely to recognize income for that second $1,000. That inventory is worthless.

- There are real costs associated with this inventory and it is important to convert it into cash as soon as possible. For example, while your business is racking up time on a project not billed out, you are still maintaining office space that you pay for, as well as paying the salaries of your staff.

- Services are unlike goods in the sense that, when you deliver a good to a customer, the value is tangible (i.e., I'm giving you a table and you're giving me $500). The value of a service is less tangible, especially when it is billed by the hour. The customer generally cannot witness the time put in first hand, so it is always important to make the value visible. If time is overlooked for a long period, the older it is, the more difficult it may be to get the customer to pay for it. The value of a service diminishes greatly in the mind of a customer the longer the time between the provision of the service and the invoice.

What's included in the inventory costs?

There are more costs of holding inventory to consider than just the purchase price of the materials or goods. Sometimes, these satellite costs can weigh down a business and damage cash flow. Consider some of the following costs of holding inventory:

- **Storage costs.** These include warehouse space, cold storage, and retail shelf space.

- **Tracking costs.** All businesses that hold inventory have some method of tracking that inventory. These systems can range from simple count sheets to point-of-sale scanners.

- **Insurance.** The inventory must be insured while being stored and also while in transit.

- **Obsolescence.** The longer inventory sits around, the more chances that a new product will come on the market and make the old inventory unsaleable.

- **Damage.** The longer inventory sits around, the more chance for damage or deterioration.

- **Theft.** Theft can occur with inventory that has no formal tracking system and also with inventories that sit in storage for a long time.

- **Opportunity cost.** Although opportunity cost isn't a hard cost (i.e., you don't have to put out money for it), it is a real cost in the sense that you could have taken the money that you invested in your inventory and used it for another revenue-generating purpose. For example, instead of having that entire inventory sitting in the warehouse, you could have invested money in advertising to bring in more customers. You may lose out on that potential revenue because you are instead holding inventory.

- **Restocking costs.** You incur certain costs every time you place an order with a supplier or every time you set up a machine to do a production run. These costs are generally fixed, regardless of the amount of inventory you order or produce. Therefore, the more you order or produce each time, the lower the overall restocking cost to the business.

- **Out-of-stock cost.** This is another soft cost rarely contemplated by smaller businesses. You can potentially lose business if you don't have stock of a certain item. Customers like to be sure that if they put the effort into visiting your store or warehouse, you will be able to provide them with what they need. If they perceive that you are frequently out of stock on the items they need, they may take their business elsewhere.

Inventory management is basically the balancing of the first seven costs above with the last two. The first seven represent the costs associated with holding too much inventory and the last two are the costs of not holding enough inventory.

Inventory management techniques

Methods of managing inventory range from the very simple to the very complex. How complex your system needs to be is determined by how much inventory you hold and how long you hold it.

Manual tracking

If you buy books and resell them at a stall at your local farmer's market, your total inventory wouldn't be high and it would turn over fairly quickly. In such a case, you can use a relatively simple inventory management system, something as simple as listing each title and quantity on a spreadsheet and then marking them off as they are sold. Sample 6 shows a tracking sheet you can use for this purpose. Note that the quantity on hand is denoted as a single stroke in the box. When the item is sold, a crossing stroke is added. When all boxes are crossed off, you are out of that item.

INVENTORY TRACKING SHEET

Code	Description										
14A	Standard coils (lg)	\	\	\	\	\	\				
12C	Line adapters	X	X	X	\	\	\	\	\	\	\
9A	Connector plugs (lg)	X	X	X	X	X	X				
9B	Connector plugs (sm)	X	\	\	\	\					
18F	Fan turrets	X	X	\	\	\	\	\	\	\	\
5B	Wrap mindens	X	X	X	X	X	X	X	X		
6A	Model strips (15")				\	\	\				
6B	Model strips (12")	X	\	\	\	\	\	\	\		
9F	Fister pipes	X	X	X	X	X	X	X	\		\
7A	Band enforcers (lg)	X	X	X	\	\	\	\			
7B	Band enforcers (sm)	X	X	X	X	X	X	X	X	X	\

The ABC management system

This system is effective for businesses that have different types of inventory and where a small quantity of the inventory represents a large portion of the total inventory cost. The ABC system requires you to break your inventory into three or more groups (Group A, B, C, etc.). Group A items are the items that cost you the most. Group C items are those that are required in great quantities but have very little value. Group B items are those in between. If we go back to our furniture-maker example, Group A might include the oak planking required for the tables. Group C would include the nails, screws, and other small hardware needed for the manufacturing process.

In this system, Group A is monitored closely as it represents a large portion of the total inventory cost. Re-order levels are kept to a minimum and inventory flow is monitored to make sure that the items are being brought into the inventory system and sent out as efficiently and effectively as possible. Group C items are monitored much less closely as they have little value and, therefore, there is little risk in keeping large quantities on hand.

Diagram 2 shows a visual example of the ABC method. Note how Group A items only represent 10 percent of the total inventory by count but represent 65 percent of the total inventory value.

Diagram 2
ABC TRACKING METHOD

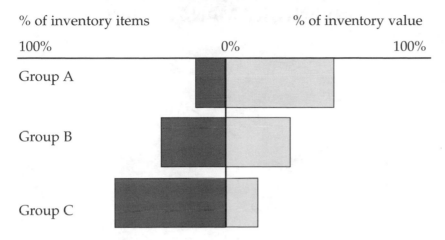

% of inventory items   % of inventory value

100%   0%   100%

Group A

Group B

Group C

Economic order quantity (EOQ) model

Although this method of inventory management is frequently used in large businesses, it is useful for smaller businesses to understand as well. The economic order quantity model graphically plots the costs of holding inventory against inventory levels. The inventory carrying costs rise and the costs of restocking the inventory fall as inventory levels rise. There is a point at which these two costs intersect, and that represents the lowest total cost. When inventory is re-ordered in the quantity that relates to this lowest cost, the business makes the most effective use of its inventory.

This seems a little complex, but when seen on the graph in Diagram 3, it makes more intuitive sense. Note that the vertical direction of the graph shows the cost in dollars (or pounds or lira) of holding inventory. The horizontal line shows the size of inventory orders.

As you order larger quantities of inventory, the carrying costs of that inventory increase (because of extra warehouse space, utilities, staffing, etc.) This increase in cost is shown by the carrying cost line that rises as you go farther to the right.

The restocking cost line gets smaller as you order larger quantities of inventory. If you place an order with your supplier for 10,000 units of an inventory item, the cost of placing the order is less than if you buy 1,000 units ten times. The same holds true for a manufacturer. If there are set-up costs associated with setting up machinery for a production run, those costs diminish with larger amounts of product put through the run.

CASE STUDY

Diagram 3
ECONOMIC ORDER QUANTITY MODEL OF INVENTORY MANAGEMENT

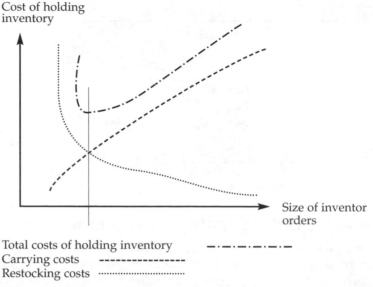

Total costs of holding inventory ⎯·⎯·⎯·⎯·⎯
Carrying costs ⎯⎯⎯⎯⎯⎯⎯
Restocking costs ·······························

The curved line at the top of the graph is the combination of the carrying cost line and the restocking cost line. You can see that the total cost of holding inventory is the lowest at the point where the other two cost lines intersect. This is the economic order quantity, or the most efficient order size of inventory for your business.

The economic order quantity is calculated using algebra, and it will not necessarily be that useful to you. However, understanding all the various costs surrounding inventory will help you to cost-effectively order and hold your inventory.

Chapter summary

➡ Inventory can be one of a business's most substantial costs.

➡ Service businesses may need to track time inventory.

➡ There are many satellite costs of holding inventory that can impact your business.

➡ Inventory management is the task of balancing the costs of holding too much inventory with the costs of not holding enough.

Accounts Receivable: The Money Coming In

In this chapter, you will learn —

- How to set your credit terms
- How to set up a collection process
- Whether factoring your receivables is a viable idea for your business
- When to get a collection agency involved
- How to monitor receivables

Because your cash flow will be tied up by your level of receivables, it's critical to actively manage your receivables and your credit policies. Make the time to understand and develop your policies and processes.

We'll start by looking at the sales and collections cycle and then we'll discuss setting up your credit policies, collecting your receivables, and monitoring your receivables account.

CASE STUDY

The sales cycle revisited

We examined the operating cycle in detail in *Bookkeepers' Boot Camp*, the first book in the *Numbers 101 for Small Business* series. Your business's operating cycle is the time it takes to complete the cash circuit; in other words, how long it takes cash to revert back into cash. A business has cash, buys (or makes) products or provides services, and gets paid for them, thereby converting cash to inventory to accounts receivable back into cash. Take a look at Diagram 1 in Chapter 5 for a reminder of what the operating cycle looks like.

The *sales cycle* is the portion of the operating cycle that occurs from the moment a sale is made to the moment cash is collected. Some activities in the sales cycle include —

- Preparing sales invoices
- Monitoring accounts receivable
- Collecting payments
- Analyzing bad debts

The "hold up" in the sales cycle is usually the accounts receivable. It represents cash that will be collected in the future, and it is critical to the health of your cash flow to collect your receivables on a timely basis.

Setting up your credit policy

Some businesses never have to worry about accounts receivable. Your local corner store, for example, won't let you buy milk and bread now and pay later. These are known as cash businesses. Businesses that deal only in payment upon receipt of the product or service have a more immediate cash flow than those that accept credit.

Why would any business extend credit terms? Because it is standard in many industries. If you will not give credit terms when all your competitors do, you will find yourself without very much business. Extending credit to customers is one way of maintaining your competitive advantage.

However, there are some real risks and costs of extending credit. First, you bear the risk that the customers will not pay. They will have received their product or service and walked away, either intentionally or due to their cash flow situation.

Second, you bear the cost of carrying the accounts receivable. This means that you have already incurred the cost of providing the product or service and you will continue to bear that cost until the customer pays you. This will most likely require you to obtain financing to fund your accounts receivable. The cost of that financing (i.e., the interest) is your cost of carrying the receivables.

The third major cost of having receivables is the cost of maintaining and monitoring the system. Receivables must be entered into your books, they must be monitored while they are outstanding, statements of account must be produced and sent to your customers, and you will have to spend time on the telephone trying to collect your overdue accounts.

In setting up your credit policies, you must balance the projected additional business you will get from providing credit terms against the costs of maintaining a receivables system. There are three main components involved in setting up your credit policies:

- Terms of sale
- Credit decisions
- Collection policies

Terms of sale

This establishes on what terms you wish to sell your product or service. For example, your terms of sale might be cash-on-delivery (COD) in which case, you will have no receivables. On the other hand, you may wish to sell with a requirement to pay in a certain number of days (common practice is 30 days).

Your terms of sale might also include incentives to pay early or penalties on paying late (or sometimes both). For example, you may wish to set 2/10 net 30 as your terms. This tells your customers that you will give them a 2 percent discount if they pay within 10 days, and that otherwise the bill is due in 30 days. This provides an incentive for your customers to pay within 10 days to receive the discount. This also benefits you, as you will get the money in the door 20 days earlier. You will need to decide if the 2 percent lost revenue is worth getting the money in sooner. In most cases where you have external financing of the receivables, it is generally worth it.

You may also set a penalty for being late. Your terms may state that the bill is due in 30 days and that 2 percent interest per month will be charged on overdue accounts. This gives your customers an incentive to pay within the 30 days and not be late. If there is no penalty for late payment, your customers have no incentive to ever pay the bill.

Explicitly state the terms of sale you set for your business on all your invoices and statements. When you meet with a new customer for the first time, you should discuss your credit policies or write them down in a "Welcome to Our Company" brochure. The more clarity you have up front about your policies, the less grief you will get later on.

Credit decisions

Another consideration in setting your credit policies is determining which customers to extend credit to. You do not necessarily have to grant credit to everyone. You may wish to find out more information about a customer (especially one who will be buying large quantities or large dollar values of goods or services from you).

It can be difficult knowing whether or not to grant credit to a customer. Especially in the start-up years, it can be difficult saying "No" to a potential customer. However, setting your credit policies will save many hours of your time and effort trying to collect from customers that don't pay. That's time that is better used for seeking out new business.

Use the five Cs of credit evaluation to determine the credit-worthiness of a customer:

- **Character.** Does the customer appear to understand the importance of paying bills on time?

- **Capacity.** Does the customer have enough cash flow to meet its debt obligations, including yours?

- **Capital.** Does the customer have a solid asset base with which to back its debts?

- **Collateral.** Does the customer have assets with which to secure the debt?

- **Conditions.** What is the financial condition of the industry that the customer is in?

The following sources will help you get information on a potential customer's credit history:

- **Financial statements.** Ask your customers for a copy of their most recent financial statements. You can then analyze their key ratios to determine their solvency. (See Chapter 4 for a full discussion of ratios.) Consider setting a standard for all your credit granting and only extending credit to those businesses whose ratios meet or exceed the standard.

- **Credit history with other suppliers.** When a customer applies for credit, you may wish to ask for references from other suppliers. Make sure you actually follow up with the references. Call the other suppliers and ask them about their relationship with the customer, including how quickly the customer usually pays the customer's purchase volumes and, in general, whether the customer is a good business to deal with.

- **Credit scoring agencies.** There are many agencies that will provide you, for a fee, with a report on the creditworthiness of a business or individual. Two of the largest in North America are Equifax (for individuals) and Dun & Bradstreet (for businesses). These agencies collect information on businesses and individuals from banks, suppliers, and other sources, and convert the information into a credit score. This score assists you in determining the future paying habits of your customer. For example, if you had a potential new customer that wanted you to ship 12 dozen computers right away, you would probably find it helpful to know how that customer has treated its other suppliers in the past. If the customer has had invoices sent to collection agencies or has unsettled and unpaid invoices with many other suppliers, you would probably think twice before selling to this business on credit. If you coupled this information with the knowledge (from your review of the customer's financial statements) that the customer's short-term liabilities are almost double the current assets, you would probably insist that the customer pay cash for the order.

Collection policies

The third major component in setting up your credit policies is to determine how you will go about collecting the receivables. How effectively you deal with overdue accounts will affect your cash flow more than almost any other management function. In a perfect world, it would be enough for you to state your credit policies on your invoice and the customer would happily pay you at the correct time. Here are some reasons why this doesn't always happen:

- The customer may simply be unscrupulous without any intention to ever pay. The sooner you are aware of this and take action, the more likely you will eventually see some cash.

- The customer may be distracted and only pay attention to the bill when he or she receives a statement of account. In this case, the sooner you get statements of account out the door, the sooner cash will come in the door.

- Some customers may be using you as a source of financing. They may routinely take 60 or 90 days to pay their suppliers, working on the premise that most suppliers will let the receivables go that long before they get serious about collection.

Take some time when setting up your business to determine your collection policy and ensure that your customers are aware of it. For example, if your terms are net 30 days, you may wish to send out a statement of account at the beginning of every month for all customers that have outstanding invoices. This will include customers whose invoices are not yet due, but it will be a gentle reminder to them of when their invoice needs to be paid.

Place a bright sticker or other indication that action needs to be taken on statements for customers with accounts over 30 days. In many cases, this will be enough to get the account paid. At 60 days overdue, you may wish to call the client directly and discuss the invoice. As much as you may not want to discuss the invoice with your customers, they will want to discuss it even less — and this may prompt them to pay the bill. At 90 days, you may wish to turn the account over to a collection agency to recover the funds. This will make your life much easier. You'll be able to concentrate on your well-paying customers and let professionals deal with the non-payors. They're good at it and they do it for a living. We will talk in more detail about collection agencies later in this chapter.

Factoring receivables

What happens if your accounts receivable are active and well paying, but just the sheer volume of the receivables is hurting your cash flow?

One answer is factoring. Factoring is popular in some industries but unheard of in others. Under conventional factoring, your receivables are discounted and sold to a lender. The lender pays you the discounted amount up front, and then assumes the responsibility for collecting the receivables. The benefit of this is that you get paid for your receivables right away. There are, however, two major potential down sides:

- It can be an expensive source of financing. If the discount is large, giving up the full amount of the receivable in the future may not be worth getting the discounted amount now.

- Your customers may view you as being in financial distress. The customer now pays the lender, not your business. This may make them think that you are insolvent or in the process of bankruptcy. It depends on the industry you operate in. In some industries, factoring is quite normal and expected.

In some cases, you may be able to pledge your receivables to the lender rather than assign them directly. This means that your customers still pay you but you agree to turn over the receipts to the lender. This keeps your customers from being aware of the transactions, but still does not address the expense issue.

Should I hire a collection agency?

We talked earlier in the chapter about what to do with seriously delinquent accounts (i.e., those over 90 days). Dealing with poor-paying customers can sap your time, energy, and soul. There's nothing worse than continually calling a customer who either ducks your calls or gives you lots of excuses or empty promises. If you're like most small business owners, you might even take it personally.

There's a lot to be said for turning over these accounts to a collection agency. Most collection agencies work on a contingency plus a small annual fee. If they are able to collect from your customer, they take a cut of it and forward the rest to you. If you really feel that you will get nothing out of the customer and you do not want them to be your customer any more, there's no risk to you. Let the professionals deal with it. If, however, you wish to maintain the customer relationship, you should think more carefully about going this route. Most customers will be annoyed that the debt went to a collection agency. They may no longer want to deal with you, either out of shame or out of anger. Many collection agencies, however, use very soft tactics in the beginning in order to try to preserve the relationship. They save the hardball stuff for the real offenders.

If you hire a collection agency for ongoing work, have a policy for turning over your accounts. For example, you might decide that everything over 90 days goes to the collection agency. You may wish to put a note on the 60-day statement warning of this result; sometimes that is enough to make the customer pay.

A collection agency can make your life substantially easier and can help you to focus on your good customers. When choosing which agency to use, find out all that you can about them. How long have they been around? Do other reputable businesses use them? What fees and charges do they have? Will they assist you in small claims court should that become necessary?

Monitoring your receivables

In Chapter 4, we talked about monitoring receivable ratios to ensure that your average collection period mirrors your credit terms. It's important to watch for changes in your average collection period because this can act as an early indicator of problems. For example, if your terms of sale are net 30 and your average collection period has traditionally hovered around 29 days, that suggests that your credit and collection policies are working. If, however, the average collection period starts to climb to 40 or 50 days, this indicates that customers are taking longer to pay and you will need to re-examine your credit and collection policies.

Another way to look at your receivables is through an aging schedule or an aged accounts receivable report. This is a listing of your accounts receivable by vendor. The receivables are sorted into aging "buckets," usually current, 30 days, 60 days, and 90 days. The percentage of receivables in each bucket is calculated. If your percentages of overdue receivables start to go up, it also indicates a problem that needs addressing. Sample 7 shows an example of an aged accounts receivable report.

Sample 7
AGED ACCOUNTS RECEIVABLES REPORT

Small Company Inc. Aged accounts receivable 29 February 2004					
Customer	Current	30 days	60 days	90 days	Total
Jim Fox	563.12		49.97		613.09
Brandywine Inc.		1,712.56			1,712.56
Merna Finlayson	197.58				197.58
J. Morgan				798.37	798.37
Baxter Box Co.	47.34	182.89	612.49	19.49	862.21
Drawton Inc.	1,983.67				1,983.67
Total	2,791.71	1,895.45	662.46	817.86	6,167.48
% of total	45	31	11	13	100

Notice that 31 percent of the receivables are 30 to 59 days old, 11 percent are 60 to 89 days old, and 13 percent are 90 days or older. In other words, 55 percent of the total receivables are overdue. If that total shot up to 65 percent, for example, you would need to examine why your customers are paying more slowly. You would adjust your policies or enforce your existing policies as needed. Even with no change in the percentages, there still appears to be a problem with collections that should be investigated.

Chapter summary

➡ Take time when you start your business to structure and formalize your credit and collection policies so that you can avoid problems later on.

➡ Credit should only be extended to those customers that meet certain criteria once you have analyzed their creditworthiness.

➡ Factoring receivables can be one method of raising short-term capital, but it can be an expensive form of financing.

➡ Monitoring your aged accounts receivables report and your receivables ratios can help you spot trouble before it can have a long-term impact on your business.

CASE STUDY

"Do you really think that doing those tiny things will make a difference?" asked Becky.

"They're not tiny things; they're critical processes," replied Vivian. "Let's run through them one more time."

"Okay," said Becky. "We're going to invoice the day after the work is done. I will monitor the aged accounts receivable list weekly and send statements monthly on the first of the month to all customers who have outstanding balances. If an account is over 30 days old, I will put a sticker on the statement bringing it to the customer's attention. At 60 days, I'll call them, and at 90 days, I send them to a collection agency."

Vivian added, "And don't forget that you are only going to take a credit application for any customer whose account is expected to exceed $1,000."

Joe crossed his arms over his chest. "It sure would be nice to get paid on time for a change. If these things help that to happen, I'm all for them."

Accounts Payable: The Money Going Out

In this chapter, you will learn —

- How to monitor due dates
- The true cost of supplier financing
- What happens if you get behind

We talked in the last chapter about the money coming in and how to make that happen faster. Now we're going to discuss the money going out and how to stretch that out longer.

We will look at the benefits and costs of supplier financing, how to set up a monitoring system for due dates, and how to minimize the cash going out.

Supplier financing

You probably don't think of your suppliers as financing your operations but if you are receiving credit terms from them, it is simply another form of lending that has a cost attached to it.

The suppliers that offer credit terms will either offer a discount for early payment or interest on overdue accounts (or both). How do you know when it's to your advantage to take advantage of these terms?

Let's look at the example of a supplier that offers the terms 2/10 net 30. As we discussed in Chapter 8, this means that if you pay the bill in 10 days, you will get a 2 percent discount, and in any event, the bill is due in 30 days. Taking advantage of this credit is free to you for 10 days. You will either pay in 10 days to take the maximum advantage of the free credit or you will pay in 30 days to get the longest possible use of cash in exchange for giving up the discount. The extra 2 percent essentially buys you an extra 20 days of credit.

Now let's look at the cost of not taking the discount. If the order was for $1,000, you would have had the opportunity to pay only $980 if you had taken the discount ($1,000 minus 2 percent). By not taking the discount, you are borrowing $980 for an extra 20 days and you are paying $20 for that privilege ($1,000 minus $980). The interest rate for the period is 2.04 percent ($20/$980 = 2.04%).

There are 18.25 20-day periods in the year (365/20). The effective annual rate (EAR) is calculated as —

$$EAR = (1 + 0.0204)^{18.25} - 1 = 44.6\%.$$

You are essentially making 44.6 percent on your money by paying 20 days early. That's a pretty good return! If your business is cash flow poor, you must weigh the strategy of stretching out your payables against the cost of doing so. In the above situation, it would be more beneficial to maintain a line of credit with the bank in order to take advantage of early payment discounts.

On the other end of the spectrum, many suppliers charge interest on overdue accounts. A common term of sale is 2 percent interest per month for each month overdue. What is the true cost of taking advantage of this form of financing? At first glance, it would appear to be 24 percent annually (2 percent X 12 months), but it is actually higher than that, due to the negative pull of compounding. The effective annual rate is actually —

$$EAR = (1 + 0.02)^{12} = 26.82\% \text{ annually}$$

It would therefore cost you 26.82 percent to use this source of financing past 30 days. That is higher than bank financing and even higher than credit card financing. You must weigh this cost against the short-term cash flow benefit of using this source of financing.

Bear in mind that your supplier is not in the business of lending money, and the only purpose of charging you interest is to encourage you to pay your bill. They would rather have you pay on time than pay them interest. If you take advantage of that situation, you may strain your relationship with that supplier.

Generally, you should pay your payables within the credit terms offered and take advantage of discounts if your cash flow allows. In order to keep track of discount and penalty dates, it's important to have an adequate payables tracking system, which we'll look at in the next section.

Tracking due dates

If you want to take advantage of supplier discounts and avoid supplier interest and penalties, you need to set up an effective payables tracking system. Most accounting software, like *MYOB* and *QuickBooks*, can be set up to monitor those critical dates and produce a warning report of upcoming deadlines. If you want to do this manually, take a look at *Bookkeepers' Boot Camp*, the first book in the *Numbers 101 for Small Business* series, for information.

Make sure you know how a supplier determines the discount date. For example, if your supplier offers a 2 percent discount for payment in 10 days, do they count the days to the date your check is dated, the date the envelope is post-marked, or the date it's received? This is important information. Many small businesses do not track this well and think they are getting the discount when, in fact, they are not. They mail out the payment on day 10 and it doesn't get credited to their account for another few days after that. Adequate tracking systems will help you find out whether or not you're getting the discount.

What happens if I fall behind?

Hitting the cash flow wall is something no one wants to think about, and good planning can help prevent that. However, even solid businesses sometimes run into unexpected cash flow problems. In this type of situation, it's critical to restrict the outflows of cash and speed up the inflows. How do you decide what to pay first and what to put off?

Earlier in the chapter, we talked about the cost of credit. There are several ways of ordering your payables to decide which ones to pay first and which ones to defer:

- Look at the comparative costs of the credit, and first pay the ones that cost the most to maintain.

- Look at which suppliers you least want to annoy. These would be the suppliers with whom you want to maintain an ongoing relationship and that you will need to order from in the future. One example is your landlord if you rent your work premises. Chronic lateness in paying your rent will probably make her less inclined to perform repairs and maintenance for you.

- Look at the potential consequences of non-payment to each supplier. For example, if you get behind on remitting your payroll taxes to the government, they have the ability to freeze your business bank account. This would effectively halt your operations and damage the business.

It's always a good idea to discuss your situation with your suppliers. Some will be more sympathetic than others, but none will be sympathetic if you just avoid them completely. Give them some general time frames for probable payment but don't commit yourself to a payment plan that you can't maintain. You may wish to provide them with post-dated checks as a show of good faith, but make sure you have the money to cover them. The only thing worse than a customer who pays late is a customer who pays late and bounces checks!

Chapter summary

➡ It's important to understand the true costs of taking advantage of your suppliers' payment terms.

➡ It is almost always to your advantage to take advantage of supplier discounts, if cash flow permits.

➡ A good accounting system will track the due dates of your payables and warn you of impending deadlines.

➡ If you hit the cash flow wall, review your payables and order them based on penalty, supplier relationship management, and consequences.

Buying New Things: Are They Going to Pay for Themselves?

In this chapter, you will learn —

- The difference between an investment purchase and an expense

- How to set a capital expenditures budget

- How to analyze decisions

- How to calculate the benefit of a new purchase

- How to monitor production improvements

Deciding whether to invest in new equipment or machinery is difficult for businesses of all sizes. The most difficult piece of the puzzle is figuring out whether future projected cash flows from the investment more than offset the up-front cost of the equipment. This process is called capital budgeting and large businesses use elaborate methods and equations to figure out when something is a good investment.

Smaller businesses can benefit from understanding these strategies as well. We will start by looking at how to analyze potential investment decisions and then take a look at the discounted cash flow decision model. We will then discuss how to evaluate projects against one another, because you don't have an unlimited supply of money to invest.

Projected benefits

Businesses evaluate potential investments all the time, usually without any formal decision mechanism. "Should I pay $1,000 to run that ad in the paper?", "Should I buy that new printing press?", and "Should I get a new delivery truck?" are all examples of this type of from-the-hip decision making.

You will be able to make the best decisions for your business if you formalize the process of capital acquisitions. For example, you could decide that every purchase over a certain dollar amount (say $1,000) must be run through this decision analysis model. This will ensure that you are making the best use of your business's limited funds.

First, let's examine the potential financial benefits of an acquisition, both immediately and over the foreseeable future. We do this by looking at the incremental increase in cash flow that the acquisition is expected to generate. We need to separate out the existing cash flows from the increase in cash flows. For example, if your business has annual cash inflows of $50,000 and the new piece of equipment is expected to boost that cash inflow to $75,000, we only want to look at the additional $25,000. The other $50,000 is going to happen whether we buy the equipment or not and therefore is irrelevant to the decision-making process.

You'll also need to examine the potential satellite effects of the acquisition. It is quite common for a new investment in capital assets to generate either good or bad satellite effects. For example, if you purchase new equipment to produce a new line of computers, you may find that sales of the new line come at the expense of sales of the older lines. You would therefore have to keep in mind the erosion of your other sales. The net projected benefit would be reduced by the expected reduction in existing cash flows.

You may also realize positive satellite effects. Producing a new product may bring new customers to your business who will buy other products from you. You should capture an estimate of these positive side effects in the net projected benefit estimate.

Now that we have the projected benefits of the investment, how do we figure out whether it's a good idea or not? We use a tool called discounted cash flows to help us.

Discounted cash flows

Discounted cash flows help us to understand if the cash inflows from the new project exceed the cash outflows. This helps us decide whether or not we want to invest in the capital asset. If the cash outflow up front is higher than the inflows over time, clearly it would not be a net benefit to purchase the asset.

Let's look at an example. A printing business is considering buying a new binding machine. The new machine will be able to produce professional quality perfect-bound books, which the business currently is unable to do. It is expected that the business will gain new customers as a result of this new capability. The increase in revenues from the new customers is expected to look like this:

Year 1	$3,100
Year 2	5,500
Year 3	7,700
Year 4	10,400
Year 5	11,250

It is also expected that the new process will have a small negative impact on current revenues, because some of the existing customers would switch from spiral binding to perfect binding. The negative impact is expected to be as follows:

Year 1	$900
Year 2	1,000
Year 3	1,050
Year 4	1,100
Year 5	1,125

The printing press costs $27,000 and has an expected useful life of five years. At the end of the five years, it will be sold for $6,500.

We now have all the cash inflows and outflows related to the project. The first step is to net the negative satellite effect from the projected revenue increase. The net projected benefit is the increase in revenues minus the negative impact on sales:

Year 1	$3,100 - 900 = $2,200
Year 2	5,500 - 1,050 = 4,450
Year 3	7,700 - 1,050 = 6,650
Year 4	10,400 - 1,100 = 9,300
Year 5	11,250 - 1,125 = 10,125

The cash inflows and outflows can be shown like this:

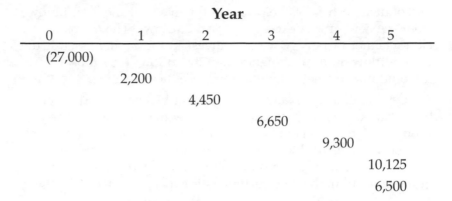

Year

0	1	2	3	4	5
(27,000)					
	2,200				
		4,450			
			6,650		
				9,300	
					10,125
					6,500

The problem when looking at these inflows and outflows is that they occur at different times. We have to spend $27,000 today and we will get a revenue stream in the future. But, for example, $9,300 four years from now is not worth as much as if it were $9,300 today. We have to wait for it.

Discounted cash flows determines the value today of cash flows in the future. That way, we can look at all the inflows and outflows as of today and see if the project will generate a net benefit.

We use the concept of the time value of money to help us. This concept states that a dollar today is worth more than a dollar tomorrow. Cash now is better than cash later. How much better?

To find that out, we need to discount all our cash flows back to today: point zero. What rate do we use to discount? There are many theories around that, but for our purposes, we will use the rate at which the business can borrow money. This is because you are taking money and buying a capital asset with it. You could have used it to pay down your existing debt but instead you used it to purchase an asset. Therefore, you are still paying interest on your existing debt.

Continuing with our example, let's say this business has existing debt at 10 percent. This is the rate we'll use to discount all our cash flows. There is a formula to calculate the present value of a dollar, but we will take the easy way and use a table. This table is found in Appendix 2. Match the interest rate (in this case, 10 percent) at the top with the periods along the side, and read off the corresponding factor for each period. To calculate how much our future cash flows are worth today, multiply each cash flow by the factor for that period.

Let's follow through the example, using a portion of the present value table reproduced below:

Period	10%
1	0.9091
2	0.8264
3	0.7513
4	0.6830
5	0.6209

We'll use these factors to bring all our cash flows back to the present time. So in Year 1, we would multiply $2,200 by 0.9091 to calculate the present value of that cash flow. The chart below has completed the calculations.

Year

0	1	2	3	4	5
(27,000.00)					
2,000.02 ◄— 2,200					
3,677.48 ◄————— 4,450					
4,996.15 ◄——————— 6,650					
6,351.90 ◄————————— 9,300					
6,286.61 ◄——————————— 10,125					
4,035.85 ◄——————————— 6,500					

(27,000.00) Total outflows

27,348.01 Total inflows

You can see from the chart that the present value of the total cash inflows is $27,348.01, which is more than the total outflow of $27,000. This means that the acquisition is a net benefit to the business and the asset should be purchased. If the total outflows were greater than the total inflows, you would decide not to invest in the asset as it would cost you more than it would bring in. An analysis of the net present value can be extremely helpful when deciding on capital expenditures.

Just to re-enforce the concepts, try the same analysis for our above business with a discount rate of 12 percent instead of 10 percent, using the table in Appendix 2. Would you still invest?

Payback

No, this is not a Mel Gibson revenge movie. Payback is another method of determining the value of an acquisition. Although it is a simpler method than the discounted cash flow method, it has a few drawbacks.

Payback looks at the length of time it takes to recover our initial investment in an acquisition or project. Let's use the example from above. Remember that our cash flow stream looks like this:

Year

0	1	2	3	4	5
(27,000)					
	2,200				
		4,450			
			6,650		
				9,300	
					10,125
					6,500
Total:	2,200	6,650	13,300	22,600	39,225

Payback simply looks at how long it takes to get back our investment of $27,000. We can see that we don't accumulate enough cash inflows until sometime in year 5. At the end of year 4, we have only recovered $22,600 of our initial investment. We must wait for the revenues in year 5 before being totally paid back. Note that with the payback method, we do not take into account the time value of money, like we do in the discounted cash flow method.

Payback is only useful when deciding among projects. For example, let's say that we were assessing another project similar to the one above, except that we achieve payback in year 3. Which one would you choose? All other things being equal, you would choose the alternate project as you get your money back into your pocket faster.

The down side of payback analysis is that it does not directly take into account the fact that a dollar later is not worth a dollar today. Another concern is that it views risky and safe projects exactly the same way.

Benchmarking

If you have many ongoing capital acquisition decisions, you may want to set a benchmark for your business, a standard that you will use to evaluate all projects. You may decide that, even though you can borrow money at 10 percent, you want all your acquisitions to return 14 percent when assessing the discounted cash flow and you want your payback to always be four years or less. This way, any new project gets compared to the standard to decide whether to invest or not.

The scarcity of resources (or "There's only so much cash")

Sometimes as a small business owner, you will face the dilemma of having to choose among investments. Even though there may be ten capital assets you could invest in and they all provide you with a positive net present value, chances are, your funds are limited. Your business only has so much money and can only borrow a limited amount of funds.

You must choose among the projects. How do you decide? There are a few considerations to keep in mind:

- **Most benefit.** You may choose to pick the project that provides the most positive net present value. This will return the most cash to you.

- **Least risk.** Some projects are going to be inherently more risky than others. For example, if you are looking at buying equipment and setting up a new division in an industry you have not operated in before, there is a fair amount of business risk. You would require your positive net present value to be quite high to compensate you for this risk. (We talk more about risk management in Chapter 11).

- **Fastest payback.** You may choose the project that gets your initial investment back in your pocket the soonest.

However you make the decision, after reading this book you will have the tools at your disposal to analyze the numbers and make a more informed choice.

CASE STUDY

"So you're saying that the compressor will pay for itself in just under a year?" asked Joe.

"That's right," said Vivian. "With the expected increase in business that you have projected, it appears to be a sound investment."

"Well, I can think of a few more things we could invest in that would bring us in more business," said Joe, reaching for the catalogue.

"Just hold your horses. If we buy the compressor, we won't have enough money for any other equipment purchases. Maybe we should look at all our alternatives, and choose the one with the shortest payback." Becky started typing in the computer.

"That's a good idea, Becky," said Vivian. "Then you will have assessed all the possibilities and chosen the right one."

Chapter summary

➡ When deciding whether or not to invest in capital assets, it's important to look at all the projected cash inflows and outflows.

➡ A new project may have both positive and negative satellite effects on current revenue. These must be factored in to the cash inflows and outflows.

➡ Discounted cash flow is one method of determining whether the benefits of a project outweigh the cost. This method discounts all cash flows back to today to take into account the time value of money.

➡ Payback is another method of analyzing a capital acquisition decision. Payback looks at how long it will take for the cash inflows to repay the initial outflow.

Chapter

11

What's Not Showing on Your Financial Statements

In this chapter, you will learn —

- What dangers lurk off your balance sheet
- How these dangers can damage your business
- How to manage off-balance sheet risk
- How to monitor your risk profile

So far, we have learned how to interpret our financial results of operations and make better decisions based on what the numbers are telling us. However, there is a hidden side of your business that you probably don't give much thought to. In the accounting world, it's called off-balance sheet risk. What that means is that risk can occur even when it's not showing as a liability on your financial statements.

The definition of risk is the possibility of danger, injury, or loss. You face many risks in your business; these may include the risk of cash shortfall, the risk of loss of revenues, the risk of loss of assets,

and the risk of lenders calling in your debt. Much of this risk can be predicted by your financial statements. We have already seen in Chapter 4 that ratio analysis can give us a good indication of risk. However, off-balance sheet risk is more difficult to detect and measure.

Generally accepted accounting practices around the world are changing to try to capture this type of risk in the notes to financial statements of large businesses. However, this only relates to businesses that have annual audits. Small businesses can still get by without reporting off-balance sheet risk.

As a small business manager, it is in your best interest to make sure that you know what risks your business faces and how to mitigate them. We will look at the "big six" off-balance sheet risks, talk about what damage they can inflict on an unsuspecting business, and consider how you can actively manage those risks. At the end of the chapter, we will put together a monitoring system that you can implement in your business to monitor your business's risk profile.

The six big risks

Your business may face one or all of the following six off-balance sheet risks. We will discuss them in no particular order.

Operating lease obligations

Capital leases are captured on your balance sheet as liabilities. However, operating leases are not. They are called off-balance sheet liabilities because you are obligated by contract to pay them, but the total liabilities under the contract do not show anywhere in the financial statements.

Typical examples of operating leases are vehicle leases, rental premises, and office machinery leases (fax machines, photocopiers, espresso machines, etc.). If the required payments are not factored into your budget report or your rolling 12-month cash flow, you may find yourself in a cash flow crunch.

Lack of adequate insurance

Most small business owners only think about insurance once a year — at renewal time. You need insurance for many things in your business, including —

- Asset loss
- Business interruption

- Death or disability of key employees
- Death or disability of the owner
- Liability to customers

It's important to have insurance to cover anything that would be catastrophic to your business and cause you severe financial pain. Worksheet 1 at the end of this chapter will help you determine your insurance needs.

Personal guarantees

Many small businesses incorporate not only for the tax advantages but also to give them some measure of protection from personal liability. This is a commendable move. It makes sense to protect your personal assets from liability in your business. However, the benefit of this "fire walling" strategy is lost if banks, lenders, or suppliers require the personal guarantee of a corporation's owners.

Frequently, lenders will only lend to new corporations if the owners will sign on as guarantors. That means that if the corporation defaults on its obligation, the lender can go after the personal assets of the owners. This can present a huge hidden risk to small business owners, especially in volatile industries.

Take some time and list every obligation for which you have given your personal guarantee. List the total amounts for which you would be personally liable should your business default. Initiate discussions with your lenders and request that the personal guarantee be released when some type of milestone is reached. For example, if your business makes all its bank loan payments on time for a 12-month period, you might be allowed to have the personal guarantee released.

Director's liability is another risk you may assume along the same line as personal guarantees. The laws for director's liability vary among jurisdictions, so you should check with your accountant and lawyer to find out what the laws are in your area. In general, director's liability laws dictate that the directors of the corporation (this will definitely be you as the owner of a small business) can be held personally accountable (i.e., liable) for losses incurred by other stakeholders in the business. This means, for example, that if you, as director, decided that you would spend the business's money on a yacht in the Bahamas instead of paying your payroll liabilities to the government, the government could say that you were negligent in your role as director and they could come after your personal assets to settle corporate debt.

Fortunately, there is insurance for directors of corporations. Directors who sit on the boards of large corporations definitely need this type of insurance but, as a small business owner, you should consider it as well.

Economic dependence

The term economic dependence is used when a business's financial health is tied to an external force beyond its control. The most frequent example of economic dependence occurs when one of your customers accounts for a significant portion of your revenues. If that customer were to take its business elsewhere, you might not be able to continue operations. The loss of that one customer would wreak irreparable damage to your business. This is frequently seen with businesses that have military contracts. The contract can be so large that the business works almost exclusively on it for one or more years. If the contract were to be pulled, it would be doubtful whether the business could continue.

Economic dependence can be a difficult risk to control, especially in the start-up years. You may only start out with a few large customers. However, it's important to make sure that you don't have "all your eggs in one basket." Diffuse the risk by constantly seeking new customers and new avenues of revenue. Then, if one customer leaves, you can carry on business as usual.

Foreign exchange exposure

Risk related to foreign exchange happens when your cash inflows are in a different currency than your cash outflows. For example, if you get all your revenue from US customers and you pay all your bills in Canadian dollars, you will be better off when the Canadian dollar falls and worse off when the Canadian dollar rises. If you have both inflows and outflows in US dollars, you are not exposed to this risk, because your revenues and expenses will rise and fall in tandem.

There are several ways to hedge this risk. One way is through currency option contracts. Let's look at an example. You are a Canadian business selling goods to a US customer in US dollars. The invoice is for US$10,000. You know that the customer will pay you US$10,000 in 60 days. However, you are concerned that the value of the US dollar will decrease over the next 60 days in comparison to the Canadian dollar. This would leave you with less money in your pocket, as you must convert the US money into Canadian money to pay your bills. The current rate of exchange at the time of sale is 1.596, which means that the value of the receivable is CDN$15,960. You estimate that the exchange rate will decline to 1.493 in 60 days, so you would really only be getting CDN$14,930. You would be worse off by CDN$1,030.

A solution is to buy a currency option on the options market to lock in your exchange rate. You would pay the option price to buy an option at somewhere in between 1.596 and 1.493. Let's say that you pay the option price of $30 to buy a "put" option at 1.582. This means that 60 days from now you have the option (but not the obligation) to sell your US$10,000 at 1.582. If the exchange rate is higher than 1.582, you will not exercise this option. It simply expires and you are short the $30 option price.

In this scenario, you win because the US dollar is stronger than you anticipated. If, however, the exchange rate falls below 1.582, you will exercise your option and will get the rate of 1.582 for your US dollars. This protects you from unfavorable changes to exchange rates. It's almost like purchasing insurance. If you don't need it, you don't benefit from it, but it's there for you if unfavorable conditions arise.

There are many more sophisticated ways of hedging foreign exchange risk, including currency swaps, forward contracts, and future contracts, but these are beyond the scope of this book. Simply be aware that any time your cash inflows and outflows are in different currencies, you are exposed to risk. Speak with your accountant to find out how best to mitigate this risk.

Interest rate exposure

Interest rate risk occurs when your debts have a floating interest rate that changes with current market conditions. For example, if you have an operating loan of $25,000 with a floating interest rate that is currently at 4.5 percent, you will be worse off if interest rates go up. Your interest payments will go up and your cash flow will go down correspondingly.

The only situation where this would not matter would be if you have a $25,000 receivable, also with a floating interest rate, currently at 4.5 percent. If this were to happen, your interest receivable and interest payable would move in tandem and there would be no risk. This perfect match is a rare occurrence, however, and most small businesses that have floating debt are at risk.

Small amounts of interest rate risk are survivable, but businesses that are exposed to greater risk use a variety of means to hedge that risk, including interest rate swaps, options, and forward

contracts, all of which are beyond the scope of this book. Speak to your accountant for more information.

Risk management for entrepreneurs

Now that you know what kinds of risk your business is exposed to, you must actively manage your risk. This will allow you to ride out the storm of changes in economic or other business conditions that are beyond your control. Use the risk profile in Worksheet 1 as an integral part of your monthly management operating plan, and update it at least quarterly.

Chapter summary

➡ Many risks that a small business faces are hidden and don't show on the balance sheet as liabilities.

➡ There are six major off-balance sheet risks: operating lease obligations, lack of insurance, personal guarantees, economic dependence, foreign exchange exposure, and interest rate exposure.

➡ There are various methods of minimizing each risk.

➡ A risk profile should be an integral part of your monthly operational plan and should be updated at least quarterly.

Worksheet 1
BUSINESS RISK PROFILE

Date:

1. Operating lease obligations

A) List all cash outflows under operating lease obligations for the next 12 months.

B) Cross-check to ensure that all payment obligations appear on the company's rolling 12-month cash flow.

2. Insurance

A) List all insurance policies, with type of insurance, amount insured, and premium.

B) List all assets that are uninsured.

C) List replacement value of all assets that are insured and cross-check them to the payout value of the insurance policies.

D) List all assets that are underinsured (i.e., if you lose them, your business will suffer and they are either not insured at all or are insured for less than replacement cost).

E) State plan and timeline for insuring assets in D) above.

3. Personal guarantees

A) List all company debts for which you have pledged personal guarantees or assets, including dollar value.

B) State plan and timeline for requesting lenders to remove personal guarantees.

4. Economic dependence

A) List your top three customers and the percentage of your annual revenues each accounts for.

B) If any of the three account for over 25 percent, list your growth objectives for the next 12 months and your plan for attaining them.

5. Foreign exchange exposure

A) What percentage of your revenues is denominated in a foreign currency?

B) What percentage of your payables is denominated in a foreign currency?

C) If either A) or B) are over 15 percent set up a meeting with your accountant to discuss mitigating your foreign currency risk. State date and time.

6. Interest rate exposure

A) List all your interest-bearing liabilities, including dollar amount owing, interest rate, and whether it is a fixed or floating rate.

B) If your floating rate debt is more than 25 percent of your total interest-bearing liabilities, set up a meeting to discuss the issues with your accountant. State date and time.

Investor and Manager: The Split Personality of the Small Business Owner

In this chapter, you will learn —

- The various hats you wear as an owner/manager

- How to separate out your job functions

- The importance of economic profit

- How you are compensated for managing your business

- What return you get on your investment in the business

This chapter is all about you — the owner and manager of your business. Up to this point, we have been concerned with the financial viability of the business: Can we keep the doors open? How do we plan for growth? How do we collect our accounts receivable more efficiently?

But there's another critical aspect of your business — you. As a business owner, you wear many hats, but the two main ones are that of manager and investor. We'll look at each of these roles separately.

The small business manager

This is the role you are most familiar with. You are in this role when you work in your business. Some of the main management functions are:

- Business planning (e.g., cash flow analysis, budgeting, growth modeling, resource planning)
- Human resource management (e.g., hiring, firing, performance evaluation)
- Supply management (e.g., ordering inventory, shipping, warehousing)
- Sales (e.g., talking to new and existing customers, advertising, dealing with delivery problems)

You could hire a manager to perform these functions for you, but most small business owners do it themselves out of financial necessity. Say, for the time being, that you will keep the manager job. How well does it pay?

Let's look at your situation. Fill in the following information:

(a) Amount of income from your business that you were taxed on last year: _____

(b) Number of hours you worked in your business last year: _____

(c) A/B = _____

Are you at least making minimum wage? If you're like most owner/managers, you are making between $1 and $3 per hour. Hardly a sustainable wage!

Why is it that small business owners are willing to put up with such a low hourly wage? Because they believe they are building something for the long term. The problem is that 80 percent of all businesses fail in the first five years, and 80 percent of the rest fail in the next five. Odds are, there will be no long term, especially for those businesses that fail to plan well.

Time and time again, I see clients in my practice who slave away at their businesses for 10 and 12 hours (or more!) a day for years without getting paid. Any money they do make gets farmed back into the business to keep it going. This takes an astronomical toll on the business owner's morale, health, and family. How long would you work for someone else and not get paid? Not very long.

When you do your cash flow projections (see Chapter 5), make sure that you include a line called "management salary" or something similar. Plan for your personal income. Not enough money in the cash flows for that? That indicates a problem. It means you are under-capitalized. It also means that you are permanently chained to your business. You couldn't hire a manager for free, so you will have to continue to do it forever.

How do you know how much you're worth as a manager? Look around your industry. Look at what your competitors are paying their managers. Look in the Help Wanted section of your local newspaper. What are the salaries being offered to managers in similar roles?

Once you have a sense of what you're worth to your business, put your pay in the cash projections and make it work. If you're in the start-up phase, you may have to borrow from a lending institution in order to cover your salary. The business must be able to cover the principal repayments on the debt as well as the interest. If it can't, you will need to look at new ways of attracting increased business. (We will look at business growth in the third book in the *Numbers 101 for Small Business* series.)

When you have planned out your salary, *pay yourself first!* This is critical. If you leave yourself until last to get paid, there's a good chance you will run out of money before you get around to it. You will make sure all other suppliers get paid because they will pick up the telephone and yell if they don't get paid. You have to treat yourself just like any other supplier — worthy of prompt payment.

When you are receiving consistent income in your personal bank account for the hours you put into your business, your outlook on the future (and most likely your stress level) will change dramatically.

The small business investor

You wear another hat in your business. It's one that you probably haven't thought about much. You are an investor in your business. You have most likely invested personal resources (e.g., cash, equipment) into the business, and like any other investment, you should get a financial return.

This has nothing to do with the hundreds of hours you spend working. This only relates to the financial resources you have expended. Let's say that when you started your business, you took $5,000 out of your savings account for start-up costs. What else could you have done with that money?

CASE STUDY

- Invested it in the stock market
- Bought a bond
- Put a down payment on investment real estate
- Loaned it to another start-up business

What would have been the benefit of doing those things? If you had invested in the stock market, you might have income on your investment in the form of capital gains or dividends. A bond would have generated interest income. Real estate will provide capital gains and rental income. A loan to another business would generate interest. In all these cases, you would be making a financial return on your $5,000.

You didn't do any of those things however. You invested in your own business. Was it a good investment decision? It is if you are making a return on that investment that is similar to other investments that carry similar levels of risk.

For example, when you invest your money in the stock market, there is no guarantee that you will get the money out that you invested. The stock market goes up and down based on many underlying indicators, some of which have nothing to do with whose stock you invest in. However, you are compensated for this risk by the possibility of substantial gains on your investment.

When you buy a bond, you bear the risk that the underlying bond issuer will not be able to repay the principal or the interest to the bondholders. The issuer needs to compensate the bondholders for that risk. If the issuer is a government, generally, it will be more stable and therefore will have to pay the bondholders a lower interest rate. If it is a corporate bond, the interest its bonds pay is dependent upon the stability of the business.

Investing in your own small business has risks too. In general, you know that the money is not liquid. In other words, it cannot be taken back by you whenever you want. It is needed for the operation of your business for a certain length of time. You also know that 80 percent of small businesses fail in the first five years and 80 percent of the ones that do survive fail in the next five years (of course, you're expecting that your business won't be one of the casualties, but it's still a risk).

So, how much return should you receive on your investment? Probably more than a government guaranteed investment and less than a junk bond. How you take that return is a question to discuss with your accountant. You can pay yourself either dividends or interest. Which way is the best will be determined by the tax laws in your particular jurisdiction.

Chapter summary

➡ As a small business owner, you wear two hats: that of manager and that of investor.

➡ It is important to be compensated for both your roles.

➡ Compensation as business manager should be commensurate with other similar roles in your industry, otherwise, you may be stuck doing it yourself forever.

➡ Compensation as investor should take into consideration the value of the investment as well as the risk of investing in a small business.

Growing Your
Business 101

In this chapter, you will learn —

- The three ways to grow your business

- How to formalize a growth plan for your business

- The difference between good growth and bad growth

- How to measure and monitor your growth plan

In this chapter, we will talk about the three ways to grow your business, how to track your progress, and what to do when things aren't working.

Many small businesses use the "splatter" approach to marketing and growth. They throw together some advertisements for the newspaper or perhaps for radio. They prepare some flashy brochures and mail them to all the potential customers in town. They take out a big advertisement in the yellow pages of the telephone book. Then they cross their fingers and hope that business floods in the door.

There are several reasons why this approach doesn't work. It's far more expensive to attract new customers than it is to keep current customers. And until you improve the way new customers are handled in your business, you may simply have more people deciding not to buy from you.

Someone once said, "I know I'm wasting half of my advertising money. I'm just not sure which half."

Let's take a look at the different ways you can grow your business.

The three methods of business growth

There are only three ways to grow your business. Any growth strategy you can think of falls into one of these three categories:

- **Attract new customers.** This is the obvious one. Get new people in the door to buy your product or service. This is the type of strategy that advertising supports.

- **Sell them more.** Another way to grow your business is to sell more to your current customers. This is a key strategy of companies like McDonald's ("Would you like fries with that?") and amazon.com ("If you liked that, you will love this"). These customers already know you and like what you have to offer. Chances are, they will like more of what you have to offer. This is also known as up selling.

- **Sell to them more often.** The second strategy focused on selling them more every time they buy from you. This strategy focuses on having them buy from you more often.

These three methods encompass all business growth strategies imaginable. However, many small business owners concentrate only on the first strategy, getting new customers. This can be dangerous for a number of reasons. First, as we mentioned earlier in the chapter, it is expensive to market to new customers. This is where the advertising budget goes. Second, new customers are not yet loyal to you. It takes time to build relationships with customers. Third, it's hard to market to a cold audience. You are trying to peddle your wares to people who do not know you or your business practices. They must take a leap of faith to buy from you.

Smart businesses focus on the customers they already have. These are the customers who have purchased from you before, know what you have to offer and like it. They know you, your business practices, and your premises. Buying from you is comfortable and familiar to them. Why not ensure that you are getting the most from these customers?

Let's look at a strategy to bolster your business using your existing customer base.

Leverage

The great thing about understanding the numbers behind your business growth strategy is that it gives you power that you wouldn't otherwise have. Making even small incremental changes in each of the three growth areas provides you with leverage. This means that the numerical result of all the changes is greater than the sum of the individual pieces. Let's look at an example:

We currently have 1,000 customers. On average, each customer spends $175 each time they buy from us. Our customers buy from us on an average of twice annually. What are our current revenues?

1,000 customers X $175 X 2 = $350,000

What would happen if we put strategies in place to make small changes in the number of customers, the average amount of each sale, and the number of times they buy from us?

Let's say we're aiming for only a 5 percent increase in the customer base, a 10 percent increase in the amount of the average transaction, and we will attract them three times a year instead of two. What's the impact on our bottom line?

Customer base: 1,000 $\longrightarrow$ 1,050

Average transaction: $175 $\longrightarrow$ $192.50

Number of visits: 2 $\longrightarrow$ 3

Our new annual revenue would be:

1,050 customers X $192.50 X 3 = $606,375

That's a 73 percent increase in bottom line revenue from small changes in each of the three areas of business growth. We haven't doubled our customer base. We haven't doubled our prices. We've simply made small incremental changes in each area that add up to a leveraged result.

Let's look at the three methods of business growth in more detail and consider how to implement and track them

Attract new customers

By how much did your customer base grow last year? If you're like many small business owners, you really have no idea. It's only when you start tracking your statistics that you get a grip on what happens when there are changes in your asset base.

Take some time and track how many active customers you have right now. If you're using an accounting program like *QuickBooks* or *Simply Accounting*, you will be able to go into the customer list and count. If you're using a manual system, you may have to go back through your invoices for last year and make a list.

Now that you have a list, put a letter beside each customer's name, either A, B, C, or D. A is for customers that buy lots from you, pay promptly, bring in other new customers, and are pleasant to deal with. These are customers you love doing business with. D customers are those who are price sensitive, complain often, and pay late or not at all. B and C are somewhere in between. This ranking gives us an idea of what types of customers we want to attract. Clearly, we only want to attract new A customers.

You may find that most of your advertising is targeting D customers. Every time you advertise that you have the lowest price, you attract price-sensitive customers. The problem with these types of customers is that you will never instill loyalty in them. The minute a competitor can come up with a lower price (and someone will always be able to do that), these customers are gone.

Now, take some time to analyze how you are going to attract new A customers. Are you in a business where trust is important? Then you will most likely get a majority of your new customers from referrals from your existing customers. Why not send a letter to your existing A customers and offer them a 10 percent discount on their next order if they bring in a referral. Oh no, you say. I can't afford to do that! Let's look at the numbers using our example from above:

Average order of existing customer	$175.00
10% discount	(17.50)
Average annual revenue from a new customer	$350.00
Lost revenue	17.50
Gained revenue	350.00
Net gain	$332.50

If you want to be more detailed, you would also count the cost of the stamp and paper for the letter. You would get even more mileage out of this strategy if you implement the other growth methods and increase the average value of each sale and the number of visits.

There are many strategies to bring new people in the door. The third book in the *Numbers 101 for Small Business* series will focus exclusively on building your business. The key point here is to track your numbers so that you better understand your business.

Sell them more

This strategy aims to increase the average value of every transaction. This is also known as up selling. The key is making sure that your customers are aware of all the other products and services you have to offer. When customers come into your gas station to pay for gas, ask if they need any oil or wiper fluid. If they come in to your restaurant and order dinner, ask them if they would like dessert. Make saying yes easy for them. Give them choices instead of expecting them to say if they want something. They might not even be thinking about buying anything but what they came for — unless you remind them.

Another method of keeping your products and services fixed in the minds of your customers is by keeping in touch on a regular basis. Send them quarterly mailings or newsletters. Give them valuable information while reminding them that you are ready and waiting to take their order.

Sell to them more often

You've now got more customers coming in the door and they're buying more when they come. Now we want to have them come in more often. Accomplishing this will be different in every industry. In the restaurant industry, for example, you can send out coupons to current customers to entice them to eat more often at your restaurant than at another. In the auto repair business, you can put together a package for customers to have a lube, oil, and filter change for a set price. Send out reminders twice a year that their car is due for this service. The possibilities are endless!

Tracking your business growth

Growing your business without tracking your results is like running a marathon without looking at the clock. It doesn't give you any indication of how you're doing and whether you're achieving your goals.

Growth benchmarks should be a part of your monthly management operating plan and you should track new customers, average revenue per customer, and average customer visits. As well, you should track where your new customers are coming from. Are they visiting your business because of an advertisement you ran?

CASE STUDY

Joe stared at the computer screen. "You mean if we increase our customer base by only 5 percent, sell 5 percent more to each customer, and see them once more per year, our revenue would go up 63 percent?"

"That's right, Joe," said Vivian. "Small incremental changes add together to make a big difference. And now you have the tools to analyze your revenue growth, so you will be able to fine-tune this plan as you go."

"This maintenance package we've set up is a great idea. Our customers get Joe to come out for two hours, and he checks all the pipes, drains the water heater, and fixes all the taps for $65.95. The best part is that we can push the service in our slow times when Joe wouldn't have any work anyway."

Or has someone referred them to you? Knowing this helps drive your growth efforts in the future.

A template for tracking your business growth can be found in Appendix 1.

Chapter summary

➡ There are only three methods of growing your business: attract new customers, sell them more, and sell to them more often.

➡ Small improvements in these three areas will yield significant increases to the bottom line.

➡ Advertising for new customers may not be the most effective method of growing your business.

➡ Tracking your growth is critical to understanding in which direction you are going.

Facing the Scary, Two-Headed Banker Monster

In this chapter, you will learn —

- How to approach a bank for financing

- What banks look for in their lending process

- How to maintain a strong relationship with your banker

- Where to look for other forms of financing

Okay. So your banker might not have two heads. She might not even be scary. But she certainly will seem frightening when you approach your bank for financing. It can be difficult interpreting what your banker wants from you or why she will or will not turn you down.

In this chapter, we will cover what a bank looks for in a borrower, how to present your business in its best light, and how to maintain a strong relationship with your banker. We will also briefly look at other sources of financing you may have overlooked.

Lending money 101

Let's pretend for the moment that you're the banker. A small business owner comes to see you to get a loan. She has been in business for almost a year now and is running into a cash flow crunch. She figures that she needs another $25,000 to get her through it. You ask to see her financial statements and she hauls out a manual general ledger to show you her neat orderly figures.

What do you want to know about this woman and this business before you part with your money?

- **Can she run a business?** You'll want to know what her business background is. How experienced is she at marketing, operational management, and bookkeeping? How is she handling the day-to-day management of the business?

- **Is this a good business?** You'll want to see her business plan and cash flow projections. How does she intend growing her business and who will she employ to implement the plan? Does she have enough staff? Is this a growing or declining industry? Is she innovative enough to make it?

- **What will she use the money for?** You'll want to know if she has a well-defined plan for the money she's asking for. Is it for capital expansion? Current operations? Will it make more money for the business?

- **Will you get your money back?** You'll want to secure your loan as much as possible to make certain that you get it back. You'll look at her financials to see what assets are on the balance sheet. You'll ask about her personal and business credit history to look at how she has treated lenders in the past. You'll look at her cash flow history and her cash flow projections to see if she is solvent enough to make loan payments.

In short, you'll want to know as much about her and her business as you can before you decide whether or not you'll lend money to her. In this situation, it appears at first glance as if she is trying to staunch the bleeding of her current cash flow with more borrowing. She would have to present a solid case for profitable growth before you would lend to her.

Your banker will look at the same things when you come to see her. She will want to know the history of the business, your personal and business financial status, and the plan for the business in the future. Some bankers have more lending discretion than others. Some have to go by certain ratios and credit score numbers, so it's helpful for you to know ahead of time what those criteria are.

Getting to know and love your banker

Go and see your banker before you need her. Have coffee with her. Chat. Find out what her lending policies and philosophies are. This meeting can save you lots of grief in the future in trying to piece together a lending proposal.

Find out what types of lending your bank prefers to do — some banks are friendlier to small business than others. Will they lend against accounts receivable or do they only lend against hard assets? What are their usual repayment terms? This is also the time to find out what your banker knows about your type of business. Although this may seem superfluous, having a solid understanding of your business will help her to make her decisions in the future (confused minds always say no). For example, if you are the owner and chief architect for a three-person architectural firm, your main assets are likely to be accounts receivable and your time inventory. Unless your banker can truly understand how this time inventory is an asset that you should be able to borrow against, you may run into problems.

The lending proposal

Now comes the time when you actually need financing from the bank. What do you take with you? You'll likely need more than your sweet and charming smile. Your banker will want answers to all the questions we've posed above. The best way to do that is to put together a professional-looking information package for her. This will serve the dual purpose of giving her everything she needs to make her decision and showing her that you are a well-organized businessperson.

If you show your banker your well-worn general ledger and your hand-scribbled notes about your plan for the money you want to borrow, chances are you will be turned down flat.

In your lending proposal you should include —

- Most recent financial statements with comparative figures back for the past five years (if you have been in business that long)
- Rolling 12-month cash flow projection
- Detailed revenue projection for the next five years
- A written section on the history of the business, its current operations, and your plans for the future
- A written plan for the use of the requested funds, with repayment figures added to the cash flow projection

- A detailed biography of you, the owner, showing your business background, the experience you have in the industry you are in, and your skills at managing an office and human resources.

Put the proposal together in a word processing program like *Microsoft Word* or *WordPerfect* (the cash flows and other spreadsheets can come out of your accounting system or from a program like *Microsoft Excel*). Print it out on clean white bond paper on a laser printer, and organize it into easy-to-access sections with numbered pages and a table of contents at the front. This should be bound together with plastic or wire binding.

Take your time with the proposal. It will show. Your local print shop can show you many options for presenting your proposal — and it should cost you practically nothing.

The care and feeding of your banker

Okay. Things have gone well. You've sweated through the meeting with the banker and after due consideration, she said yes! She didn't laugh and she didn't throw you out of her office. You have the funds in your business account and the world is good. You never have to see your banker again. Wrong. As important as it was to make a good first impression on your banker, it's every bit as important to maintain that relationship. You may need further financing in the future.

Maintain your contact with your banker. At least annually, set up a meeting with her to go over your financials and revisit your lending needs. She may have suggestions for re-arranging your borrowing to save you money in interest and fees. Tell her what you've done over the last year and how the business has grown. Bankers like to see their prophecies come true and your banker will want to know that you've made good use of the funds she has loaned you.

It should go without saying that maintaining this good relationship with your banker will be next to impossible if you miss or are late with payments. If you have had to miss a payment or two along the way, make sure that you discuss this with your banker. Don't stay silent with the fervent hope that she hasn't noticed. She will definitely have noticed.

Other dance partners

There are other lenders out there apart from your bank. They include private lenders, venture capitalists, and mortgage companies (if you have real estate to attach).

The problem with many of the alternative sources of financing is that many will assume that if you are approaching them, you have been turned down by your bank. They may be unwilling to lend to you or will charge you a much higher interest rate to compensate them for their perceived risk. Make sure you tell these lenders everything that has happened to date with your bank. If you've been turned down, tell the new lender that. They'll be able to guess as much when they run your credit history.

Mortgage companies will be able to lend to you at a low rate because they are securing their debt with real estate. Remember that although you are getting a low interest rate, you are putting that piece of real estate at risk if you miss the payments on the loan.

Your credit score

Let's end by looking at something that you should actively manage: your personal credit score and your business credit score.

Most lenders report information to credit reporting agencies. Dun & Bradstreet is the largest agency for businesses and Equifax is one of the largest one for consumers. This information may include —

- Amount of debt
- Repayment terms
- How many late payments there have been
- If any debt has been sent to a collection agency
- A whole host of other information about you that you may not have thought anyone has access to

This information is calculated into a credit score. This score tells lenders what the overall likelihood is of you defaulting on the loan. Things that can bring down your score are —

- Late or missed payments (especially on credit cards)
- Too much credit card debt
- Too much revolving debt (i.e., debt that doesn't have to be paid down, like lines of credit)
- Collections registered against you (even if they were later paid)
- Too many inquiries on your credit report

The last bullet may seem counter-intuitive, but if you have several lenders at the same time vying for your business and they all run credit histories on you, it damages your score. This is supposed to

CASE STUDY

stop people from credit shopping, but it has the effect of not allowing you to see what other offers are out there. Make sure you tell each lender who else you have approached because they will be able to see it in your credit history.

There are rules about who can access this information about you. In general, you must give written permission for someone to "run a bureau" on you. Most lenders will require you to give that permission before they will consider a loan.

You are allowed to see what's in your credit report and you should have one run on yourself at least annually. It's important to make sure that the information is accurate and up to date. Some agencies will also give you your score for a fee. This is a worthwhile number to know and I recommend you do that. To find an agency, check out the yellow pages in your telephone book under "credit agencies."

Take some time and understand what's on your credit report and how lenders view what's there. If there's something on your report that is inaccurate, call the reporting agency and find out what their procedures are for correcting errors. The time you spend understanding your credit history is time well spent.

Chapter summary

➡ You should meet with your banker before you need her so that you can understand her bank's lending policies.

➡ When you are ready to seek financing, take some time and put together a professional-looking lending proposal for the bank.

➡ Keep in touch with your banker at least annually and keep her up to date on the growth of your business and the use of the funds.

➡ Understand your credit history. Have a reporting agency run a history on you at least annually so that you can ensure the information is accurate and up to date.

Chapter
15

Managing Debt

In this chapter, you will learn —

- How to analyze your business's existing debt load
- How to re-arrange your financing to benefit from changes in market interest rates
- How to reduce the risk of leverage
- How to pay down your debt in the most efficient way
- How to monitor your debt

Debt. It's the word many small business owners hate to hear. It's a reality for most businesses however to incur debt to finance operations, at least in the start-up years. Although many small businesses are denied credit in the first few years of operation, others have bankers and credit card companies begging for their business, especially those businesses whose owners have substantial personal assets to attach.

"We've got to get rid of all this credit card debt, Joe," Becky said, rubbing at the creases in her forehead. It was almost midnight and Joe and Becky were sitting at the kitchen table, fine tuning the business plan.

"Why? We get to write it off." Joe poured himself another coffee. "Besides, the bank won't refinance our credit card, remember?"

"Part of the reason they won't loan us anymore is because we have all this credit card debt." She paused as she realized the dual truth and absurdity of the statement. "And even if we get to expense the interest for tax purposes, we still have to pay the interest. We're still worse off."

Joe looked over the budget for the next 12 months. "We've already budgeted in the payments. So we should be fine."

"That's only the interest, Joe. At that rate, we'll carry this debt forever. Let's see if we can work out a payment strategy for all our debt."

I hear the following from small business owners every day:

"It doesn't matter. I get to write it off."

"You can't operate in this industry without a big line of credit."

"I need a corporate credit card to take my customers out to lunch."

"You have to spend money to make money."

All these arguments are superficial and speak more to our penchant for overspending than anything else.

The first statement, "It's a write off..." is the most tenacious argument of the lot. Many small business owners think that because something is tax deductible, it's free. If you look at it on paper, however, you will see the foolishness of the premise. Let's say, for example, that you spent $1,000 in interest on a loan. The $1,000 is certainly deductible from your income. At a 25 percent corporate tax rate, this would give you $250 in tax savings. *But you still had to fork over $1,000!* You are still out of pocket by the difference of $750. It's critical to get a grip on your debt picture and how much interest you are paying. This will help you plan and grow more effectively in the future.

We've already looked at debt from the bank's perspective in the previous chapter. In this chapter, we will look at how to measure and manage the debt.

Understanding debt service

Debt service represents the amount of money it costs a business to maintain or "service" its debt. It includes both interest and principal payments required for a business to remain on side with its lenders' covenants or agreements.

Some of your debt may require only interest payments while some might be a blend of interest and principal repayments.

The purpose of incurring debt in any business (both the corner store and General Motors) is to generate more revenue. This is called leverage. The theory is that with more capital available to a business, it can buy more equipment or invest in more promotional activities in order to bring more customers in the door. In many cases however, a lack of understanding of these principles hides the fact that debt is simply being used to prolong the agony of an unprofitable business. Understanding your total debt service will help you to determine whether your indebtedness is helping you earn revenues.

Let's use an example. A business has annual revenues of $75,000. It currently has an outstanding loan with the bank that requires monthly payments of $250, or $3,000 annually. It enters into a loan for $25,000 at 10 percent for five years. The blended principal and interest payments are $531.18 per month, or $6,374 annually. The new loan is intended to pay for the purchase of new technology. It is expected that the new technology will draw new customers and that there will be a 10 percent increase in revenue annually. There are two ways to analyze the situation.

Debt service ratio

Like any other ratio, the debt service ratio only has meaning when compared over time. In this situation, we would compare the ratio of debt to revenue under the current situation and under the new debt scheme.

The basic calculation for the debt service ratio (DSR) is —

Total debt payments/Revenues

Currently:

DSR = $3,000/$75,000 = 0.04 : 1 (or 4%)

Under the new scenario:

Total debt payments will be $3,000 + $6,374 = $9,374

Total revenue will be $75,000 plus 10% = $82,500

DSR = $9,374/$82,500 = 0.11 : 1 or (11%)

At first glance, it looks as if this is a bad situation. Our debt service ratio went from 4 percent to 11 percent. However, there's one more step in our analysis. We need to compare this ratio to our maximum acceptable debt service ratio.

We know that we will be paying an extra $6,374 a year for five years under the new scenario. We also know that we will be getting an extra $7,500 a year in expected revenues. Therefore, the maximum additional debt service we would be willing to pay is $7,500. If we paid more than that, then we're worse off than before because the debt is costing us more than the increase in revenue. In order to know if we're better off or worse off, we need to calculate the maximum acceptable debt service ratio and compare it to our ratio we calculated above.

Total debt service = $3,000 + $7,500 = $10,500

Total revenue = $82,500

DSR = $10,500/$82,500 = 0.13 : 1 (or 13%)

The maximum we would accept is 0.13 : 1 and under our proposed scenario, the debt service ratio is 0.11 : 1, so we know we are under the maximum. This proposed financial change is therefore a good one for the business.

Payback

The second way to analyze whether the debt is helping your business earn revenues is to look at how long it will take to "pay back" the business for the cost of the new debt.

We know that we have to pay out $6,374 a year for the next five years. That's a total of $31,870. We also know that we will get $7,500 a year in new business (potentially forever). So, how long will it take to make back the $31,870 in cost?

Payback = $31,870/$7,500 = 4.2 years

This says that it will take 4.2 years to cover the costs of the loan. This analysis is most helpful when you are considering a few different scenarios. You would calculate payback under each scenario and the one with the earliest payback is the best opportunity.

How do I calculate my cost of borrowing?

A useful measure of your business's debt is to look at the overall cost of borrowing. Comparing the blended cost of borrowing over time tells you whether it is becoming more or less expensive for the business to acquire capital.

You may have financing from several different sources:

- Bank loans
- Lines of credit
- Credit cards
- Capital leases
- Suppliers
- The government

Let's take a look at each one of these in turn.

Bank loans

Banks usually loan money for certain specific items rather than for ongoing operations. Bank loans can finance start-up costs, new equipment, research and development costs, or other tangible investments.

Bank loans are usually paid back over a fixed time frame with equal monthly instalments representing both interest and principal repayments. The interest rate on these loans is largely dependent on whether the bank is able to secure the loan with tangible assets of the business. For example, if the bank has loaned a business $25,000 for new machinery, it will put in the loan agreement a provision that, should the business default, the bank will seize the equipment. The bank could then sell the equipment and recover its money. This lessens the risk to the bank of extending the loan and it will therefore charge a lower interest rate. Loans can also be secured by a general security agreement, which gives the bank a blanket guarantee on all the assets of the business.

Lines of credit

A bank or trust company can also extend a line of credit to a business. The bank determines the lending limit for the business's current needs and that amount is available to use in increments as needed. In many cases, it's directly tied to the business's bank account so that when a business writes a check, it's taken from the line of credit, and when it makes a deposit, it tops the line of credit back up.

A line of credit is usually unsecured, or may be secured by a general security agreement. The funds are usually used for smoothing cash flow; most often needed in the cash flow deficit months and replenished in the cash flow positive months.

The line of credit generally requires interest-only repayments, which are deducted from the business's bank account. The principal is rarely fully repaid, as a line of credit is a semi-permanent method of financing.

Credit cards

Many small business owners are often proud the day they receive their first corporate credit card in the mail. To them, it represents the validity of the business. However, credit cards present the same dangers to businesses as they do to individuals.

Credit cards generally have a requirement that 3 percent of the principal balance is paid monthly, but because you can then take it back up to its limit, you are essentially only required to pay the interest. The interest rate charged on balances kept on credit cards is exceedingly high, usually in the 18 percent to 21 percent range. Corporate cards can sometimes offer "benefits" such as air miles or money toward a new car. These types of "reward" cards generally have higher annual fees and higher interest rates than other types of cards. There can also be tax implications of using these rewards for your own personal use. Check with your accountant.

Capital leases

Capital leases have proliferated in the past 20 years as a method of financing equipment purchases. These leases are generally offered by the equipment manufacturer or a leasing company and work much the same way as a bank loan. Monthly payments are required that blend interest and principal repayments for a fixed period of time. At the end of that period, either the equipment belongs to the lessee or the lessee can buy it for nominal price.

Capital leases are usually easier to qualify for than a bank loan and they are always secured by the equipment that the lease is financing.

Suppliers

Businesses do not often think of their suppliers as a source of financing, but if you carry a balance on your account and you are charged interest, this is a means of financing. Instead of taking a bank loan to pay the supplier, you let the supplier finance you.

Supplier financing is usually the most expensive form of credit available. If a supplier has 2 percent per month interest on overdue balances, this actually represents 26.82 percent annual interest due to the negative power of compounding.

The government

If you have outstanding debts to the government, such as income taxes, retail taxes collected, or payroll taxes, you will be charged interest (and perhaps penalties). This is also a (usually unintentional) form of financing.

It's important to understand the total cost of your debt from all sources. You can do this by calculating a blended interest rate from all your current debt. Let's look at an example.

A business has several different sources of financing:

- A bank loan with a current balance of $14,912 and an interest rate of 8.5 percent.
- A capital lease for computer equipment with a balance of $5,387 and an interest rate of 11.4 percent.
- Payroll arrears owed to the government in the amount of $6,754. Interest rate per the statements is 10 percent.

- A corporate credit card with a balance of $12,769 and an interest rate of 18.5 percent.

To calculate the blended cost of debt, we simply multiply each interest rate by the proportion of its related debt to the total debt. In the above example, it would look like this:

Type	Amount ($)	% of total	Interest rate %	Blended
Bank loan	14,912	37.5	8.5	3.2
Capital lease	5,387	13.5	11.4	1.5
Payroll arrears	6,754	17.0	10.0	1.7
Credit card	12,769	32.0	18.5	5.9
Total	**39,822**	**100.0**		**12.3**

The weighted average cost of debt is 12.3 percent in this example. So, what does this tell us? Not much, by itself. It's only when we look at the weighted average cost of debt over time that we are able to see if our interest rates are going up or down. If our blended rate is going up, for example, it could mean that we are beginning to have solvency issues. It means that our newer debt is at a higher rate than our existing debt. Lenders may be more hesitant to lend to us and we may be seeking financing from more unconventional (and more expensive) sources.

The danger of leverage

Many "Make Millions with Your Small Business" books will talk about leverage and "good" debt versus "bad" debt. They argue that it takes money to make money and that virtually all businesses borrow. "Good" debt (they say) allows you to leverage your funds to earn more income. For example, if you can attract $50,000 worth of new business by buying a $30,000 machine on credit, you would be farther ahead to do so.

What these "gurus" don't tell you is this simple fact:

DEBT = RISK

It's not exactly rocket science, I grant you, but it is critical information to keep in mind, nonetheless. In our above example, what happens if you don't get the increase in business you were expecting? The debt is still there. You can't tell the bank, "Sorry, I can't pay you back until I get this new business in the door." When your business is indebted to a bank, mortgage company, or other lender, you are at risk of default and of the debt being called and your assets seized. Think of it this way: only businesses that have debt declare bankruptcy. If you didn't have any debt and you wanted to wind up your business, you would simply close the doors.

Another danger that many small business owners don't think about is that many lenders require the personal guarantees of the owners and may even require you to put up your home as security. Now, not only are your business assets at risk, but everything you own personally as well. Clearly, this increases the risk of entering into credit agreements.

I'm certainly not recommending that you never borrow money. However, you need to understand the following every time you engage in credit:

- What is the purpose of this borrowing?
- Am I getting the best interest rate possible?
- What does the revised stream of cash flows look like with the new debt?
- Do I have a plan to retire this debt?
- Do I have to pledge any personal assets to get this credit?

Once you have satisfied yourself that you have done the required background work to understand your business strategy, then you can enter into the agreement with confidence.

The debt diet plan

Like a fat diet that sheds unwanted pounds, the debt diet sheds unwanted credit. There are three stages to the plan: analyze, project, and act.

Analyze

In this stage, you will sit down and look at your business's debt burden. Don't forget to include the hidden sources of financing we talked about earlier in the chapter. Make sure you are aware of all the repayment terms and interest rates involved, as well as any hidden fees. For example, many lines of credit have monthly maintenance fees that should be included in your cost of debt.

Make three lists of all of your business's debt:

- Debt that is secured by assets of the business
- Debt that is secured by personal assets of the owners
- Debt that is unsecured

For each list, write down the debt in interest rate order, from highest to lowest. The highest interest rate debt that is not secured by any asset is your first target to eradicate. This will frequently be credit card debt.

Now, let's go to the next step.

Project

In this stage, we look at the cash outflows related to each one of the debts under the current scenario. Ideally, each source of debt will have its own line on your cash flow projection, so this information should be easy to access. One thing you will probably notice is that your highest interest, unsecured debt is also the debt with no fixed repayment terms. This means that, as long as you are paying the interest, you can happily be mired in debt at 16 percent to 21 percent forever! This makes lenders extremely happy.

The goal in this phase is to work out the paydown of all debt for the business. Some loans will have set repayment terms, such as five years of monthly payments, but for those that are lines of credit or credit cards, you will have to work out the cash flow required to pay them off. As we discussed above, you should first pay off the highest interest rate debt. Once the cash flows have been adjusted for the new repayment schedules, it's time to act.

Act

Now it's time to pay down that debt! Review the cash flow budget each month to ensure that you are still able to make the paydown. Resist the urge to use credit cards or dip into the line of credit unless it's necessary. This is really no different than managing your personal credit. The faster you pay it down, the less interest you will pay and the more funds you will have to put toward the principal.

To help you stay on your credit diet, review the balance sheet every month and watch the total liabilities line, which should be shrinking. The smaller the total liabilities in your business, the more solid footing you will be on.

CASE STUDY

Joe leaned back in his chair. "You really think we can pay off all that credit card debt in 12 months?"

"That's what the cash flows are telling us," Becky said. "But, you're going to have to use the card more carefully. All our purchases should be planned out in advance. If you really need the card for something, we'll decide on it together and I'll prepay the credit card for that expense."

"You can do that?" Joe asked.

"It's a little trick Vivian taught me. It lets you still have the convenience of a credit card but avoid all the interest."

"I think that's a great idea," said Joe.

"She also told me that if we get this credit card mess looked after, the bank will look at us more seriously in 12 months. We'll be able to structure the rest of our debt better."

Chapter summary

➡ Business debt can be as dangerous as personal debt if left unchecked.

➡ Debt produces risk, which can harm your business or your personal assets, if you have secured the loan with them.

➡ Calculate your debt service ratio as part of your monthly management plan.

➡ High interest, unsecured debt usually has no repayment terms. It's the most dangerous kind of debt if you do not make a plan to pay it down.

Chapter 16

Compensating Employees

In this chapter, you will learn —

- How to calculate the value of your employees
- How to set compensation rates for your employees
- How to give performance-based compensation
- How to conduct performance evaluations
- How to measure and monitor performance

Human resource management can be one of the most difficult tasks for a small business owner. More likely than not, you, as a small business owner, have never received any kind of training in hiring, firing, and managing employees.

This chapter will look at how to value and compensate your employees. Spending time working on the compensation process provides dual benefits: it makes your employees stay longer (because you are paying them what they're worth) and it makes you more money (because you are paying them based on their performance).

Human resource management is an important and separate skill from all others you perform in your business. The goal of this chapter is to give you an overview of the compensation process and guide you to paying your employees what they're worth. For more information on human resource planning, check out *The HR Book*, another book in the Self-Counsel Press series.

What are your employees worth to you?

Office Assistant

Busy sales office requires an energetic individual with working experience in Excel, Word, and Quick-Books. The successful applicant must possess:

- *Minimum 2 years' experience in an accounting role*
- *Ability to work in a fast-paced environment*
- *Excellent customer service skills*

You've decided it's time to hire somebody. Great! Now how much are you going to pay him? Minimum wage? Twelve dollars an hour? What about benefits?

Deciding how much to pay an employee is an art. There are many considerations to keep in mind, including what value the employee is to your business. Every employee contributes to the bottom line in some fashion.

In the above example, you have decided it's time to hire an administration assistant to help with answering the telephones, filing, and bookkeeping. You may not think of someone in that role as contributing to the bottom line, but they do. The time that you are not answering the telephones, filing, and bookkeeping you can now spend on attracting new customers, marketing, and strategic planning.

The day that you hire your first employee, you are leveraging yourself. You are creating more potential growth than would otherwise be possible.

You can determine the value to the business of an employee in much the same manner as for a capital asset acquisition. You will be paying money out (wages) over time in order to get future revenue streams (the increase in business you will now be able to bring in). You will be getting value from the employee as long as the future inflows are more than the outflows.

What are your employees worth to someone else?

Although it's important for you to analyze the value of the employee to your particular business, a stronger determinant of value is what they're worth to your competitors. What use is knowing that the new bookkeeper is worth $7 an hour to you when he would be able to get $15 an hour from another employer? If you offered him $7, he either wouldn't take the job or wouldn't stay very long.

Market forces drive wage rates and you'll have to pay a competitive wage to stay afloat. How do you know what other employers are paying? Here are some ideas —

- Review the want ads in your local paper for a few weeks. Get a sense of what skills are being asked for. Many of the ads will show the hourly rate being offered.

- Call your local temporary help agency. They should be able to give you some idea of the going rate for certain skill sets (although they might also try to convince you that you don't need to hire someone on permanently; a temp would be a better choice).

- Network with other business owners. Find out what they pay their staff.

- Certain industries have published wage data for all levels of work in that industry. Consider subscribing to one of those services if applicable.

Benefits

As you're going through the process of determining what the market value is of your new employee, look at what benefits are generally offered. Some of the standard benefit packages include —

- Prescription drugs
- Dental
- Short-term disability
- Long-term disability
- Group term life insurance

Benefits are important to most employees and they will take that into consideration as they decide which position to take.

Find a good insurance agent that deals with small business group plans. Go over the costs with them and consider offering your employee a benefits package on top of his salary. (Make sure you put the cost of the insurance into your monthly budget).

Sick days

The ability to take days off sick is another benefit offered by many employers. It allows employees paid time off when they are sick or have a family emergency (and is legally required in many jurisdictions). Standards vary but in general, six sick days per year are usual.

You do not have to budget any extra cost into your cash flow for this. You will simply pay your employees when they are off sick. The only cost to you is lost productivity.

Performance-based compensation: Paying for value

There was a time when an employer would pay employees an hourly wage or weekly salary, the employee would put in eight hours a day, and that would be it.

The problem with that scenario is that the goals of the employee are not necessarily aligned with the goals of the employer. The employee wants to exchange the required labor for the amount of money that the job pays. There is no benefit to the employee of working harder, being more efficient, or coming up with new ways to do things.

On the other hand, the employer's objectives are to make money and grow the business. These conflicting objectives can cause problems. In the late 1990s, a new compensation model emerged, one that pays employees to do the "right things" for the business. This model is called variable pay, performance-based pay, or a host of other titles that all mean the same thing.

Performance-based pay is based on the premise that an employee will do what he is compensated to do. A portion of the total compensation package will be based upon clear, agreed-to criteria. The employee will receive regular performance evaluations and the variable pay component will be based on that assessment.

In order for a performance-based compensation system to work, it needs to have the following:

- **Clearly defined requirements.** The employees have to know exactly what is expected of them.
- **Controllable objectives.** The employees have to be able to control the criteria upon which they are being evaluated. For

example, it would be pointless (and demoralizing) to compensate employees based on net income if they have no control over net income. On the other hand, if employees are responsible for the expense budget, it would make sense to compensate them partially on control over that budget.

- **Objectives that are in line with the overall business plan.** It's important that the variable pay criteria fit in with the overall plan of the business.

- **Simplicity.** If the criteria are too complicated to remember on a day-to-day basis, employees will not remember the plan as they do their jobs, thereby making it ineffective.

The performance evaluation process

Once you have set the performance criteria, you will need to determine how they are to be measured. The measures should be as objective as possible and easy to understand. For example, if the criterion is, "Answers the telephone using the company script," the measurement should be a percentage of overheard telephone calls that were correctly answered.

Many performance evaluation systems use numerical scoring systems to make the process easier. A final score in a certain range would mean 100 percent of the variable pay. Lesser scores would mean lesser percentages of the total variable pay. Again, it's critical that employees understand the process, otherwise it may seem arbitrary and pointless to them.

How often should you evaluate your employees? At a bare minimum, annually. However, it makes some sense to do it as often as monthly or quarterly as it keeps the job requirements firmly fixed in employees' minds. This makes it easier for them to weave the requirements into their day-to-day performance.

Once the performance evaluation has been completed, meet with your employees one on one to go over the evaluation. Allow time for them to give their input into the process as well. This time together should be free of distraction, so consider going off-site somewhere or at least into a room with no telephones. Making sure that you will not be disturbed reinforces to your employees that you take this process seriously and most likely, so will they.

At the end of the evaluation, draw up an action plan with your employees, outlining areas to work on and specific steps that they will take to improve that particular area of performance. Let them develop the action plan. Your role here is just to guide and assist.

CASE STUDY

"Wow," said Joe. "I never had this type of performance evaluation at any job I ever worked at. If I had, I probably would have worked a whole lot harder. Are we sure we can afford to pay the employee a performance bonus?"

"If the employee does what's necessary to achieve the bonus, we will have more revenue. His performance bonus will come out of that revenue."

"Let's start working on the ad now," Joe said excitedly.

If the employees develop the solutions, there is a much higher probability that they will implement those solutions.

Keeping tabs on employee performance

The employee evaluation process is ongoing. It's not something to jam into a desk drawer and haul out every three months. It's important to monitor employee performance throughout the evaluation period and make notes with specific dates and times, not only of issues that need to be addressed but also of the great things your employees are doing. Reinforcing positive behavior will pay you dividends.

Another important concept is ongoing feedback. Employees should never be surprised by a performance evaluation. If there are any serious breaches of performance, they should be discussed with the employee immediately and not saved up for the performance evaluation. If there are small things that you feel should be addressed, do it as you go. Give the employee the opportunity to correct problems before the formal performance evaluation.

Sample 8 is the actual performance evaluation I use in my accounting practice. Many of the questions might seem to be geared toward professional employees, but we have the same standards for everyone who works in our practice. Remember that your performance evaluation system should be tailored to your business, your employees, and your business plan.

Chapter summary

➡ It's important to consider not only what your employees are worth to your business, but also what they would be worth to other businesses.

➡ Benefit packages are a standard part of most employee compensation arrangements.

➡ Performance-based compensation is emerging as an effective way to align the goals of the employee with the goals of the employer.

➡ Performance evaluations should be prepared on a regular basis, and action steps should be developed by the employee with help from you.

Sample 8
QUARTERLY PERFORMANCE REVIEW

The composite score of this appraisal will determine the bonus level and will be applied as follows:

Score Bonus

0.00 – 4.99	0%
5.00 – 5.50	10%
5.51 – 6.00	20%
6.01 – 6.50	30%
6.51 – 7.00	40%
7.01 – 7.50	50%
7.51 – 8.00	60%
8.01 – 8.50	70%
8.51 – 9.00	80%
9.01 – 9.50	90%
9.51 – 10.00	100%

Name of employee being assessed: _____

The following scale will be used for the evaluation:

- 9 – 10 *An exceptional skill:* This individual consistently exceeds behavior and skills expectations in this area

- 7 – 8 *A strength:* This individual meets most and exceeds some of the behavior and skills expectations in this area

- 5 – 6 *Appropriate skill level:* This individual meets a majority of the behavior and skills expectations in this area. There is a generally positive perspective toward responsibilities

- 3 – 4 *Not a strength:* This individual meets some behavior and skills expectations in this area, but sometimes falls short

- 1 – 2 *Least skilled:* This individual consistently fails to reach behavior and skills expectations in this area

- N/A Not applicable or not observed

Sample 8 — Continued

Work performance and individual skills

- Gets the job done right the first time N/A 1 2 3 4 5 6 7 8 9 10
- Completes work in a timely manner N/A 1 2 3 4 5 6 7 8 9 10
- Completes work accurately N/A 1 2 3 4 5 6 7 8 9 10
- Effectively works within rules and policies N/A 1 2 3 4 5 6 7 8 9 10
- Makes timely decisions N/A 1 2 3 4 5 6 7 8 9 10
- Has good verbal communication skills N/A 1 2 3 4 5 6 7 8 9 10
- Has good written communication skills N/A 1 2 3 4 5 6 7 8 9 10
- Technical skills are up to date N/A 1 2 3 4 5 6 7 8 9 10
- Writing is neat and legible N/A 1 2 3 4 5 6 7 8 9 10
- Work is organized and complete N/A 1 2 3 4 5 6 7 8 9 10
- Recognizes problems and identifies underlying causes N/A 1 2 3 4 5 6 7 8 9 10
- Has good strategic skills N/A 1 2 3 4 5 6 7 8 9 10
- Is persistent in reaching goals N/A 1 2 3 4 5 6 7 8 9 10
- Is effective at working within time limits N/A 1 2 3 4 5 6 7 8 9 10
- Knows how to prioritize work N/A 1 2 3 4 5 6 7 8 9 10
- Develops effective systems and improves processes N/A 1 2 3 4 5 6 7 8 9 10
- Keeps a clean organized work area N/A 1 2 3 4 5 6 7 8 9 10
- Brings expertise to the job N/A 1 2 3 4 5 6 7 8 9 10
- Keeps knowledge up to date by reading, researching, etc. N/A 1 2 3 4 5 6 7 8 9 10
- Coaches, motivates, and helps develop others N/A 1 2 3 4 5 6 7 8 9 10
- Is trustworthy, open, and honest N/A 1 2 3 4 5 6 7 8 9 10
- Is prompt N/A 1 2 3 4 5 6 7 8 9 10
- Has a positive outlook N/A 1 2 3 4 5 6 7 8 9 10

Total points for this section: _____

Sample 8 — Continued

Client services

- Treats clients like business partners   N/A 1 2 3 4 5 6 7 8 9 10
- Identifies, understands, and responds to appropriate needs of clients   N/A 1 2 3 4 5 6 7 8 9 10
- Presents ideas clearly and simply   N/A 1 2 3 4 5 6 7 8 9 10
- Listens attentively to clients   N/A 1 2 3 4 5 6 7 8 9 10
- Solicits and provides effective feedback   N/A 1 2 3 4 5 6 7 8 9 10
- Uses the company telephone protocol   N/A 1 2 3 4 5 6 7 8 9 10
- Provides awesome service; goes that extra mile to do things right   N/A 1 2 3 4 5 6 7 8 9 10
- Is friendly and courteous to clients   N/A 1 2 3 4 5 6 7 8 9 10
- Knows client's business   N/A 1 2 3 4 5 6 7 8 9 10
- Replies promptly to client requests   N/A 1 2 3 4 5 6 7 8 9 10
- Looks after clients in a timely manner   N/A 1 2 3 4 5 6 7 8 9 10
- Develops systems for better client services   N/A 1 2 3 4 5 6 7 8 9 10
- Keeps others informed about client needs   N/A 1 2 3 4 5 6 7 8 9 10
- Balances client requests with business requirements   N/A 1 2 3 4 5 6 7 8 9 10

Total points for this section: _____

Teamwork

- Supports the team's goals   N/A 1 2 3 4 5 6 7 8 9 10
- Puts the interests of the team
  before self   N/A 1 2 3 4 5 6 7 8 9 10
- Builds consensus and shares
  relevant information   N/A 1 2 3 4 5 6 7 8 9 10
- Treats others fairly   N/A 1 2 3 4 5 6 7 8 9 10
- Takes responsibility for own actions N/A 1 2 3 4 5 6 7 8 9 10
- Does their part to get things done   N/A 1 2 3 4 5 6 7 8 9 10

Total points for this section: _____

Management and leadership skills

- Manages resources effectively   N/A 1 2 3 4 5 6 7 8 9 10
- Takes initiative to make things
  happen   N/A 1 2 3 4 5 6 7 8 9 10
- Takes informed, calculated risks   N/A 1 2 3 4 5 6 7 8 9 10
- Makes well-reasoned, timely
  decisions   N/A 1 2 3 4 5 6 7 8 9 10
- Follows through to deliver results   N/A 1 2 3 4 5 6 7 8 9 10
- Communicates and sets clear
  expectations   N/A 1 2 3 4 5 6 7 8 9 10
- Anticipates and prepares for change N/A 1 2 3 4 5 6 7 8 9 10
- Has people skills; is fair, honest,
  dependable, and approachable   N/A 1 2 3 4 5 6 7 8 9 10
- Provides supportive and guiding
  leadership; does not try to control   N/A 1 2 3 4 5 6 7 8 9 10
- Delegates duties skillfully   N/A 1 2 3 4 5 6 7 8 9 10
- Organizes and prioritizes work   N/A 1 2 3 4 5 6 7 8 9 10
- Visionary; sees the big picture   N/A 1 2 3 4 5 6 7 8 9 10
- Applies fairness to any action   N/A 1 2 3 4 5 6 7 8 9 10
- Coaches and develops team   N/A 1 2 3 4 5 6 7 8 9 10

Total points for this section: _____

Sample 8 — Continued

Business development

- Actively seeks new clients   N/A 1 2 3 4 5 6 7 8 9 10
- Maintains required networks   N/A 1 2 3 4 5 6 7 8 9 10
- Provides input to business
  development strategy   N/A 1 2 3 4 5 6 7 8 9 10
- Suggests new services to
  provide to clients   N/A 1 2 3 4 5 6 7 8 9 10
- Learns new skills to assist in
  company growth   N/A 1 2 3 4 5 6 7 8 9 10

Total points for this section: _____

Innovation

- Constantly benchmarks
  "best practices"   N/A 1 2 3 4 5 6 7 8 9 10
- Performs frequent process review   N/A 1 2 3 4 5 6 7 8 9 10
- Solicits process improvement
  feedback   N/A 1 2 3 4 5 6 7 8 9 10
- Suggests new goals for team growth   N/A 1 2 3 4 5 6 7 8 9 10
- Researches better ways to do things   N/A 1 2 3 4 5 6 7 8 9 10
- Creates systems and procedures
  to make jobs easier   N/A 1 2 3 4 5 6 7 8 9 10
- Presents strategic ideas in order to
  improve organization and service   N/A 1 2 3 4 5 6 7 8 9 10

Total points for this section _____

Scoring

Total points from all sections/Total questions answered
= Average score

_____ / _____ = _____

Bonus level achieved: _____

Pulling It All Together:
The Planning Cycle

In this chapter, you will learn —

- The basic planning cycle
- How to set up your management planning and control procedures
- How to monitor your plan and adjust it as you go
- How to automate your plan so that it happens without you

So far, we've looked at all the major aspects of collecting the results of your business activities and monitoring them on an ongoing basis. Now, we need to step back and look at the planning and control process as a whole. Our goal is to set up a system to collect, monitor, and report on the critical information that you need to run your business successfully.

The planning cycle

Now that we know what we're tracking, we need to know how, when, and how often to track it, and most important, what to do with the information.

A business's planning cycle looks like this:

Plan——▶Control——▶ Grow——▶Fine tune——▶Plan

Notice that we start with planning. Too few small businesses plan adequately before they start up. In fact, in North America, small business owners spend more time researching and planning for a new car purchase than they do for their business start-up. That's a frightening statistic! It's also why more than 80 percent of all small businesses fail in the first five years and 80 percent of the rest fail within the next five years.

Think of it this way: A business is like a sailing ship and the goal is to find riches beyond the owner's wildest dreams on a far-away jungle coast. We have two ship captains: J.H. Lazy and F.W. Planner.

Lazy's attitude is that one can never tell where the ship will end up. Many external factors can influence the direction: wind speed, storms, ocean currents, broken navigational equipment. Lazy's plan is to just set out and see where the ship ends up. He rationalizes that he can always plot a more accurate course later, if he has to. Besides, who has all that time to waste looking at maps, plotting courses, and making sure the ship is on course? He's never run into major trouble before and doesn't expect to now.

Planner, on the other hand, knows that in order to achieve his goal, he must know where he's going, how fast the ship is likely to get there, and what to do with the riches when he finds them.

While Lazy has already sailed, Planner lays out his navigational charts and carefully goes over them with his advisors and his crew. He plots the most direct course, ensuring that he avoids shallow water and the section of the ocean most likely to be hit by devastating storms. He makes sure that his crew is aware of the plans and that they alert him if they veer off their course by more than six degrees. They will also monitor the sky for signs of an impending storm so that there is time to batten down the hatches. He strengthens the aft hold with forged iron to be able to carry the weight of the gold he expects to be returning with. Planner has met with his bankers and has made a plan for investing the gold when he returns.

Which ship do you think reached the gold first? Which ship is better off if both of them hit stormy seas? The answer, of course, is Planner and his crew, because they have taken the time to envision and plan for the ultimate goal. If that doesn't convince you of the importance of planning, consider this: If both voyages have to be financed by lenders, which voyage is more likely to get the money? Bingo!

Planning

Every business should start with a plan. The fourth book in the *Numbers 101 for Small Business* series will delve deeper into business start-ups. For now, let's assume that you made your initial plan when you started your business. Your plan should include the following pieces that we've covered in previous chapters:

- Projected revenues and expenses for at least a 24-month period
- Projected cash flow statement
- Target ratios
- Break-even and capacity calculations
- A capital replacement budget
- A list of critical success factors and their related key performance indicators
- An employee compensation and evaluation strategy
- A promotion strategy with timelines

There are many ways to put together this information. Appendix 1 provides a manual template for you to fill out in the book or to photocopy and assemble in any format that makes sense for you. You can also go to <www.numbers101.com> to download a free *Microsoft Excel* template.

Once you have determined what information you need, you must decide how often you need it. Some information, such as wastage, employee productivity, and sales, you may need weekly. Other information, such as a full budget analysis, cash flow, and product returns, you may need only monthly. And, of course, at the end of the fiscal year, you will need the full package of financial information.

Control

The next step in the process is controlling the actual performance of the business. There are as many ways of collecting and controlling the information as there are for planning. Every business will tailor the information flows to its unique needs. What follows is one method of preparing a monthly management operating plan.

The flash report

Some of the information needs to be available to you quickly and easily. Every week you will want to view this information so that you have early warning if your business is starting to derail. It's much easier to make alterations to a ship's course when it has only been off-course for a week, than after a month. What information do you need to see weekly? That's up to you. Some common weekly statistics for small businesses are —

- Weekly sales
- Average number of days for receivables
- Employee productivity
- Aged receivables
- Aged payables
- Working capital ratio

Once you have determined what information you need to see weekly, set up a format so that it can be gathered quickly and as automatically as possible. If you have office staff in your business, teach them how to gather the information. As the manager, your goal is to only have to view the information and make plans based on it. Of course, if you are a one-person show, you will not have this luxury and will have to pull together the information yourself.

Ultimately, your weekly flash report should boil down to a one-page-at-a-glance summary of whether or not you are on target. If you have weekly team meetings, this is good information to present so that everyone is aware of the larger picture. Get one of your staff to present the weekly flash report at a team meeting. This gives your team a more in-depth understanding of the planning process and the business itself.

The monthly management operating plan

You will also want to see the bulk of your management information on a monthly basis. The typical monthly management operating plan would include —

- A monthly budget showing actual versus planned
- A monthly cash flow statement showing actual versus planned
- Ratio analysis including turnover and capital ratios
- An analysis of all actual key performance indicators compared to the plan
- A synopsis of the external and internal business environment and how it has affected the business
- A thorough analysis of employee productivity
- A summary of promotional efforts and their measurable impact on results

Again, it's important to involve your staff in the process. They may have insights that you cannot see as to the causes of derailment.

Growth

It is only now, after you have a good handle on your business's operations, that you should focus on growth. Many small businesses are so concerned right from the start about growing that they do not know what impact the growth is having on their business. Without a plan, new customers can suck a business dry, absorbing more resources than they are adding revenue. Growth must be profitable and sustainable. For a more detailed discussion on business growth, check out Chapter 13.

Fine tuning

Now that your business has set its course, focused on the goal, and tracked its progress, it's time to make some minor adjustments to the path it's on. Once you have several months or years of data to work with, operational patterns will emerge. For example, you may find that every year, there is a major dip in revenues in April. This seasonality may not have been apparent from the outset. If it is something that you expect will continue, you can alter your plan to reflect that reality. You can also focus your promotional activities to produce benefits during that slow time.

By this time, you will also have a track record of measuring and monitoring the impact of changes on your business. For example, you may have discovered that a 10 percent increase in your print advertising budget will result in a 12 percent increase in sales, or that a "bonus item" promotion results in 100 new orders every time, or that buying a new piece of equipment will result in a productivity increase of 15 percent. You will be able to precisely target your efforts with the skill of a surgeon rather than that of a lumberjack.

Fine tuning is an ongoing process that involves measurement, comparison, and adjustment. It is a continual refinement of the machine that is your business. Ultimately, your job is that of skilled mechanic and your goal is to one day have the machine run without you. That's why you are spending time building in self-diagnostic tools and gauges.

Planning

Notice that we end up back at the planning stage, thus completing the cycle. Once your company has progressed through an entire business cycle, it's time to plan again. It's a continual process of bettering your business.

The planning and control processes are what set apart outstanding businesses from ordinary ones. Do you want to be in the 96 percent that fail or the 4 percent that flourish?

Chapter summary

➡ The major steps to managing your business are to plan your future financial performance, control your actual performance, grow your business, and fine-tune the plan.

➡ Set up a monthly management operating plan to assess results.

➡ Learn the "story" that your business is telling you; understand the financial peaks and ebbs and what they mean.

The Monthly Management Operating Plan

Throughout this book, we have emphasized the need to track your financial results in detail. The worksheets on the following pages provide a template for tracking your results on a monthly basis. This plan is only a guideline and you should tailor it to suit your needs.

If you would like to customize the plan, visit <www. numbers101.com>, where you will find the material available as downloadable *Microsoft Excel* files.

Use the following worksheets to form the basis of your monthly management operating plan:

- **Monthly planning meeting notes.** This form can be used to keep your monthly management meeting on track. It lets you assign different staff to present the key items and designates responsibility for following up on action items.

- **Performance highlights.**

- **Management discussion and analysis.**

- **Monthly financial reports.** Insert the current month's balance sheet, income statement, and cash flow statement, with comparisons to both budget and the same month in the prior year.
- **Rolling 12-month budget.** Update and insert the rolling 12-month budget.
- **Rolling 12-month cash flow projection.** Update and insert the 12-month cash flow projection.
- **Key performance indicators.**

Monthly planning meeting notes

Date of meeting:

Time:

Those attending:

	Agenda item	Presented by	Action items	Deadline	Responsibility
1	Review of last meeting's action items				
2	Performance highlights				
3	Management discussion and analysis				
4	Climate analysis				
5	Customer feedback				
6	Other business				

Performance highlights

Month ended: _____

	Current year	Previous year	% change
Revenue			
Cost of sales			
Net income			
New customers			
No. of transactions			
Current ratio			
Other measure:			

Management discussion and analysis

Month ended _____

1   What we did exceptionally well this month:

2   What we missed target on:

3   What changed in our operating environment:

4   What are our main focuses in the coming month:

5   What indicators will alert us to problems:

Balance sheet

Income statement

Cash flow statement

12-month budget

12-month cash flow projection

Key performance indicators

Month ended _____

(choose the four that are most important to your business)

			Current month	Previous month	Previous year

Solvency or liquidity ratios

1	Current ratio	current assets/current liabilities			
2	Total debt ratio	total debts/total assets			

Asset and debt management ratios

3	Inventory turnover	cost of goods sold/inventory			
4	Sales turnover	sales/accounts receivable			
5	Payables turnover	cost of goods sold/accounts payable			

Profitability ratios

6	Profit margin	net profit/sales			
7	Return on assets	net profit/total assets			
8	Return on investment	normalized net profit/invested capital			

numbers
101 for
SMALL BUSINESS

Appendix

2

Appendix 2 —
Present Value of $1

PRESENT VALUE OF $1

PV TABLE

Discount Rate Period	1%	2%	3%	4%	5%	6%	7%	8%	9%	10%	12%	14%	16%	18%	20%	25%
1	0.9901	0.9804	0.9709	0.9615	0.9524	0.9434	0.9346	0.9259	0.9174	0.9091	0.8929	0.8772	0.8621	0.8475	0.8333	0.8000
2	0.9803	0.9612	0.9426	0.9246	0.9070	0.8900	0.8734	0.8573	0.8417	0.8264	0.7972	0.7695	0.7432	0.7182	0.6944	0.6400
3	0.9706	0.9423	0.9151	0.8890	0.8638	0.8396	0.8163	0.7938	0.7722	0.7513	0.7118	0.6750	0.6407	0.6086	0.5787	0.5120
4	0.9610	0.9238	0.8885	0.8548	0.8227	0.7921	0.7629	0.7350	0.7084	0.6830	0.6355	0.5921	0.5523	0.5158	0.4823	0.4096
5	0.9515	0.9057	0.8626	0.8219	0.7835	0.7473	0.7130	0.6806	0.6499	0.6209	0.5674	0.5194	0.4761	0.4371	0.4019	0.3277
6	0.9420	0.8880	0.8375	0.7903	0.7462	0.7050	0.6663	0.6302	0.5963	0.5645	0.5066	0.4556	0.4104	0.3704	0.3349	0.2621
7	0.9327	0.8706	0.8131	0.7599	0.7107	0.6651	0.6227	0.5835	0.5470	0.5132	0.4523	0.3996	0.3538	0.3139	0.2791	0.2097
8	0.9235	0.8535	0.7894	0.7307	0.6768	0.6274	0.5820	0.5403	0.5019	0.4665	0.4039	0.3506	0.3050	0.2660	0.2326	0.1678
9	0.9143	0.8368	0.7664	0.7026	0.6446	0.5919	0.5439	0.5002	0.4604	0.4241	0.3606	0.3075	0.2630	0.2255	0.1938	0.1342
10	0.9053	0.8203	0.7441	0.6756	0.6139	0.5584	0.5083	0.4632	0.4224	0.3855	0.3220	0.2697	0.2267	0.1911	0.1615	0.1074
11	0.8963	0.8043	0.7224	0.6496	0.5847	0.5268	0.4751	0.4289	0.3875	0.3505	0.2875	0.2366	0.1954	0.1619	0.1346	0.0859
12	0.8874	0.7885	0.7014	0.6246	0.5568	0.4970	0.4440	0.3971	0.3555	0.3186	0.2567	0.2076	0.1685	0.1372	0.1122	0.0687
13	0.8787	0.7730	0.6810	0.6006	0.5303	0.4688	0.4150	0.3677	0.3262	0.2897	0.2292	0.1821	0.1452	0.1163	0.0935	0.0550
14	0.8700	0.7579	0.6611	0.5775	0.5051	0.4423	0.3878	0.3405	0.2992	0.2633	0.2046	0.1597	0.1252	0.0985	0.0779	0.0440
15	0.8613	0.7430	0.6419	0.5553	0.4810	0.4173	0.3624	0.3152	0.2745	0.2394	0.1827	0.1401	0.1079	0.0835	0.0649	0.0352
16	0.8528	0.7284	0.6232	0.5339	0.4581	0.3936	0.3387	0.2919	0.2519	0.2176	0.1631	0.1229	0.0930	0.0708	0.0541	0.0281
17	0.8444	0.7142	0.6050	0.5134	0.4363	0.3714	0.3166	0.2703	0.2311	0.1978	0.1456	0.1078	0.0802	0.0600	0.0451	0.0225
18	0.8360	0.7002	0.5874	0.4936	0.4155	0.3503	0.2959	0.2502	0.2120	0.1799	0.1300	0.0946	0.0691	0.0508	0.0376	0.0180
19	0.8277	0.6864	0.5703	0.4746	0.3957	0.3305	0.2765	0.2317	0.1945	0.1635	0.1161	0.0829	0.0596	0.0431	0.0313	0.0144
20	0.8195	0.6730	0.5537	0.4564	0.3769	0.3118	0.2584	0.2145	0.1784	0.1486	0.1037	0.0728	0.0514	0.0365	0.0261	0.0115
21	0.8114	0.6598	0.5375	0.4388	0.3589	0.2942	0.2415	0.1987	0.1637	0.1351	0.0926	0.0638	0.0443	0.0309	0.0217	0.0092
22	0.8034	0.6468	0.5219	0.4220	0.3418	0.2775	0.2257	0.1839	0.1502	0.1228	0.0826	0.0560	0.0382	0.0262	0.0181	0.0074
23	0.7954	0.6342	0.5067	0.4057	0.3256	0.2618	0.2109	0.1703	0.1378	0.1117	0.0738	0.0491	0.0329	0.0222	0.0151	0.0059
24	0.7876	0.6217	0.4919	0.3901	0.3101	0.2470	0.1971	0.1577	0.1264	0.1015	0.0659	0.0431	0.0284	0.0188	0.0126	0.0047

Appendix 3 — Resources for the Growing Business

www.numbers101.com

Our official Web site that is packed full of articles, advice, and business tools such as cash flow spreadsheets, templates, and links.

www.aicpa.org

The official Web site of the American Institute of Certified Public Accountants. Here you can find out what qualifications CPA's are required to have and how to find a CPA in your state.

www.cica.ca

The official Web site of the Canadian Institute of Chartered Accountants.

www.cma-canada.org

The official Web site of CMA Canada.

www.sba.gov

US Small Business Administration — lots of great resources for small businesses. Mostly US focused but useful for all companies.

www.cfib.ca

Canadian Federation of Independent Business. CFIB is an advocacy group for small businesses. They lobby the government for legislative changes that will assist businesses and their owners. On the Web site are lease-versus-buy calculators, downloadable publications, and other resources.

http://sme.ic.gc.ca

Performance Plus from Industry Canada. A great Web site for businesses from all countries. Shows you how your business stacks up with others in your industry.

www.bcentral.com

Microsoft Small Business Resources. Do they want to sell your stuff? Of course! In addition, this Web site also offers great articles on marketing, promotion, and other business matters.

www.toolkit.cch.com

CCH Business Owner's Toolkit. Great tools and resources including sample business documents, checklists, and government forms.

www.inc.com

The online presence of *Inc. magazine*. Here you will find great articles, tools, and calculators to help your business grow.

www.self-counsel.com

Online shopping for a wide variety of business titles (including this one!).

Must-read Books

There are literally thousands of books on every aspect of business, from start up to management to marketing. There are however, some books that have stood the test of time, and which, in my humble opinion, should be rendered dog-eared and tattered by every small-business owner. You can buy these books at almost any bookstore, or you can visit <www.numbers101.com> to find links to an online retailer in your country. Please note: these books are not in any particular order.

Built to Last: Successful Habits of Visionary Companies by James C. Collins (New York: HarperBusiness, 1994)

This book looks at companies that have stood the test of time and that have not only survived but also flourished while their competitors have fallen by the wayside. Learn how you can structure your business the same way to ensure that it's around a hundred years from now.

The e-Myth Revisited by Michael E. Gerber (New York, N.Y.: HarperBusiness, 1995)

This powerful book has changed the lives of hundreds of thousands of small-business owners. Gerber shows you that being able to do the things your business does (cut hair, design buildings, fly airplanes) does not necessarily mean that you have the skills to manage a business. He shows you how to work *on* instead of just *in* your business.

Extraordinary Guarantees: A New Way to Build Quality Throughout Your Company & Ensure Satisfaction for Your Customers by Christopher W Hart (New York: Amacom, 1993)

An unusual take on "the customer is always right" philosophy. This book looks at the benefits of making the buying decision risk-free for your customers.

Guerrilla Marketing by Jay Levinson (Boston: Houghton Mifflin, 1998)

Every business owner, large and small, wants information on how to market effectively at a low (or no) cost. This book, along with the others in the series, gives hands-on advice to readers on how to gain media attention and market their companies.

Marketing Your Services: For People Who Hate to Sell by Rick Crandall (New York: McGraw-Hill, 2003)

In my opinion, this is one of the best books on marketing services. It shows you how to focus on building relationships instead of selling. If you think you're paying too much for advertising space and you want to get "free" advertising, this is the book for you!

Multiple Streams of Income by Robert Allen (New York: Wiley, 2000)

This book is applicable to all areas of a business owner's life. It takes a holistic view of the entrepreneur's life and shows the necessity of having several sources of income flowing into your bank account to help you survive financial risk.

The One-Minute Manager by Kenneth Blanchard (New York: Morrow, 1982)

This book is an easy read, but a crucial one. It contains the parable of a young man in search of world-class management skills. It covers goal-setting, motivating, training, praising, and reprimanding employees. The book also explains the organizational science behind the reasons that such simple techniques work so effectively.

The 80/20 Principle by Richard Koch (New York: Currency, 1998)

This is the book that first showed us how 80 percent of our success comes from 20 percent of our effort. Every business owner should read this to find out how to achieve more with less!

The Pursuit of Wow: Every Person's Guide to Topsy-Turvy Times by Tom Peters (New York: Vintage Books, 1994)

Do you stand out from your competitors? Do your customers say "Wow!" every time they interact with you? Tom Peters shows you why it's critical to excel at customer service to survive.

The Seven Habits of Highly Effective People by Stephen R. Covey (New York: Simon and Schuster, 1989)

Covey has studied the habits that are common among the world's most successful people and has distilled them down into integrated principles. A fantastic guide to living with fairness, integrity, honesty, and human dignity- principles that will set you and your business apart.

Who Moved My Cheese?: An Amazing Way to Deal with Change in Your Work and Your Life by Spencer Johnson (New York: G.P. Putnam's Sons, 1998)

This quick read (only 96 pages) uses the metaphor of mice in a box who always know where their cheese is. But what happens when the cheese is moved? It is an outstanding look at change management and how to deal with the surprises life brings us all.

Glossary

Accounting: The cyclical recording and reporting of a business's financial transactions and the analysis of the business's financial statements.

Accounts payable (also called **trade payables**): The amounts owed by a business to its suppliers or vendors for goods and services purchased on credit.

Accounts receivable: The amounts owed to an entity from its customers for goods or services provided on credit.

Accrued liabilities (also called **accrued expenses**): The amounts owed by an entity to its suppliers or employees that relate to the current period but for which it has not yet been invoiced.

Accumulated depreciation: The total amount of depreciation taken on a capital asset to date over its lifetime. The accumulated depreciation is recorded on the balance sheet as a contra account (see definition below), reducing the total original cost of the asset. The net of the original cost and the accumulated depreciation is known as the net book value of the capital asset.

Accrual accounting: A method of accounting in which income and expenses are recorded in the periods in which they occur, not necessarily the periods in which cash is exchanged. Accrual accounting is based on the matching principle.

Allowance for doubtful accounts (AFDA): A balance sheet account that captures management's best estimate of the total of the potentially uncollectible accounts receivable *at any particular point in time.* AFDA is a contra account to the accounts receivable account.

Amortization: A term sometimes used interchangeably with depreciation, but more likely in reference to the depreciation on intangible assets, such as goodwill and incorporation costs.

Asset: Something owned that is of measurable value to the owner both in the present as well as in future periods.

Auditor: An accountant outside of a business who performs specific procedures to give the users of the financial statements comfort regarding the accuracy and completeness of the numbers.

Audit report: The single-page statement prepared by an auditor summarizing the audit procedures performed, the scope of the audit, and the opinion of the auditor regarding the accuracy and completeness of the numbers.

Bad debts: The estimated amount of credit sales that have become questionable as to collectibility *in the current period.*

Balance sheet: One of the three major financial statements of a business. The balance sheet displays everything of a measurable financial value that is owned and owed by the company.

Bank reconciliation: The process of comparing and reporting differences between the bank balance on the bank statement and the bank balance in the ledger.

Book value: The value of assets, liabilities, and equity recorded on the balance sheet of a business. Book value may differ (sometimes substantially) from replacement cost or market value.

Budgeting: The process of planning and projecting revenues, expenses, and capital expenditures for future fiscal periods.

Capital assets: The tangible operating assets of a business. These assets generally provide the business with operating capacity as opposed to being held for resale. They have a relatively long life.

Capital lease obligations: The present value of all amounts owing under a capital lease contract. A capital lease is a lease in which the rights and responsibilities of ownership have passed to the lessee.

Capital stock: The units of ownership of a corporation, issued by certificate.

Cash basis accounting: A method of accounting in which financial transactions are recognized in the period in which cash transfers, not necessarily the period to which that event relates. This method is generally not allowed by generally accepted accounting policies (GAAP).

Cash flow: The inflows to and outflows from a business, regardless of the source.

Cash flow statement (also known as the statement of changes in financial position): One of the three major financial statements of a business. The cash flow statement, in its most general terms, shows why there is an increase or decrease in cash during the year. These increases and decreases are summarized into operating, financing, and investing activities.

Certified public accountant (CPA): A widely recognized professional accounting designation in the United States. To be a CPA, one must meet educational and experience requirements, as well as pass a uniform examination to qualify for a state license to practice.

Chartered accountant (CP): A widely recognized professional accounting designation in Canada, the UK, and Australia. A CA must meet educational and experience requirements and pass a uniform examination to be able to hold a public accounting license. Requirements vary between the countries as the designation is administered by different professional regulatory bodies.

Certified management accountant (CMA): A professional accounting designation widely recognized in the United States and Canada. CMAs must also pass rigorous standards before attaining the designation: however, the focus of training is more on internal management practices as opposed to public accounting.

Certified general accountant (CGA): Another professional accounting designation in Canada that requires candidates to meet certain standards before being granted the designation.

Chart of accounts: The set of accounts used by a business that make up its general ledger. These accounts are standard to that particular organization, and all transactions must be recorded using these standard accounts unless a change is granted by management.

Closing the books: The process of ending the accounting period (usually the year) in which the balances of all revenue and expense accounts are transferred to increase or decrease the retained earnings balance. The closing procedure allows the income statement to "start fresh" for the new year.

Common stock: Represents the controlling shares of the company. The common stockholders are usually the only shareholders who have the right to vote on issues important to the survival and direction of the corporation. Common stock is required to be issued by the corporation (someone has to control the company). Upon the dissolution of the corporation, the common shareholders are generally the last to receive any net assets of the company.

Compound interest: Interest earned on your interest. You earn compound interest when you leave your interest in an investment. During the next period, you earn interest on both your principal and the reinvested interest.

Contra account: An account that nets off the balance of another account.

Controller (comptroller): The "big cheese" accountant in an organization. The controller oversees all accounting functions and sometimes operates as the company's chief financial officer.

Cooking the books: The process of making the financial results look pretty. Although there are many acceptable choices that can be made with respect to accounting policies, "cooking the books" generally involves fraudulent methods of recording non-existent transactions or transactions with values different from what is being recorded.

Corporation: One of the three main forms of business ownership (sole proprietorship and partnership are the other two). A corporation is the only type of business entity that is legally separate from its owners: it is itself a legal entity. Corporate ownership is shown through the issue of share certificates (see **Common stock**).

Cost accounting: An older term for management accounting. Cost accounting is usually more narrowly defined as accounting for the costs of manufacturing goods and apportioning them to the correct products in the correct periods.

Cost of goods sold: The purchase or manufacturing costs of the goods that were sold during a particular period. The costs related to the goods not yet sold are accounted for in inventory on the balance sheet.

Creditor: A person or other business that has loaned money or extended credit to a company.

Current assets: A category of assets on the balance sheet that represents cash and assets that are expected to be converted into cash within one year.

Current liabilities: A category of liabilities on the balance sheet that represents financial obligations that are expected to be settled within one year.

Debits and credits: Accounting terminology representing the increases and decreases in ledger accounts. Debits represent increases to assets and expenses, and decreases to liabilities, revenues, and equity accounts. Credits represent increases to liabilities, revenues and equity accounts, and decreases to assets and expenses.

Debt: The amounts owed by a business to outside persons or businesses. It is sometimes more narrowly defined as to exclude accounts payable and include only loans that have fixed interest rates and repayment schedules.

Declining balance method: An accelerated method of depreciation that results in more depreciation being taken in earlier periods.

Deferred revenue: Represents revenue received in advance of services performed or product delivered. It is a liability on the balance sheet because the business has an obligation to perform the service or deliver the product.

Depreciation expense: The portion of capital assets that have been recognized in expenses for the current operating period.

Dividends: The portion of earnings (either current or retained from prior periods) that have been distributed out to the shareholders in the current operating period.

Double-entry bookkeeping: The method of bookkeeping first documented in 1494 that recognizes that each financial transaction affects at least two balances simultaneously.

Double-declining balance method: Another accelerated depreciation method.

Earnings: A term usually used interchangeably with net income (i.e., revenues less expenses).

Extraordinary gains and losses: Increases or decreases in net income from sources not directly related to the operating capacity of the business. These are events that are not expected to recur.

Fair market value: An approximation of the worth of an asset if sold in an open market environment.

Financial Accounting Standards Board (FASB): The issuer of generally accepted accounting principles in the United States and its most authoritative standard-setting body.

Financial statements: The main summary financial reports produced by a business's accounting and bookkeeping system. The three major financial statements are the balance sheet, the income statement, and the cash flow statement.

Financing activities: One of the three major summary categories on the cash flow statement. Financing activities are those transactions between a business and its sources of funding. It includes the borrowing and repayment of debt, issue and retraction of share capital, and the payment of dividends.

First-in, first-out (FIFO): A method of inventory valuation by which the inventory items are tracked in and out in date order. When a sale is made, it is the cost of the oldest items in inventory that is applied to Cost of Goods Sold account, and it is the cost of the more recent purchases that remain in inventory.

Fixed assets: An older term for capital assets (see **Capital assets**).

FOB destination: A method of determining who owns goods in transit: the business or the business's customers or suppliers. If something is shipped FOB destination, title to the goods does not pass to the purchaser until the goods have reached the purchaser's premises.

FOB shipping point: A method of determining who owns goods in transit: the business or the business's customers or suppliers. If something is shipped FOB shipping point, title to the goods passes to the purchaser when the goods leave the vendor's premises.

General ledger: The grouping of accounts used by a business. Also, the book where the main summary records are kept for each balance sheet and income statement item.

General journal: A detailed record of all financial transactions of a business. The general journal is summarized and entered as net increases and decreases to the accounts in the general ledger.

Generally accepted accounting principles (GAAP): The collection of standards and practices required to be used by businesses to record and present the results of their financial activities and their records of what they own and what they owe. GAAP can be different between industries and between countries.

Goodwill: In the general sense, goodwill represents the intangible asset that a business possesses by virtue of its good name in the community, strong and loyal customer list, and brand-name recognition. In its more narrowly defined accounting sense, goodwill represents the intangible value that has been paid for when a company purchases another company. This is the only type of goodwill that generates accounting recognition. It is carried as an asset on the balance sheet.

Gross income: Another term for revenues.

Gross margin: Represents revenues minus the cost of goods sold in the period.

Income statement: One of the three major financial statements of a business. (The balance sheet and the cash flow statement are the other two.) The income statement shows operating activity over an operating period from revenues, expenses, and extraordinary gains and losses.

Income tax payable: The total of the income taxes that have not yet been remitted to the government but are due at the end of the year. This total would include income taxes in arrears if there were any.

Insolvent: A term used to describe a business that does not have enough assets to meet its debt obligations in the short term. Insolvency can lead to bankruptcy if not corrected quickly.

Internal control: Represents the procedures set up in a business to prevent errors and fraudulent activity.

Inventory: Goods held for resale that remain unsold at the end of an operating period. In a manufacturing environment, inventory includes raw materials, goods in the process of being made, and finished goods. In certain service industries, inventory includes time spent on customer activities but not yet billed out.

Investing activities: One of the three major summary categories on the cash flow statement. Investing activities include the purchase and sale of capital assets, including land, buildings, equipment, furniture and fixtures.

Investments: Usually, long-term investments in other companies, as opposed to the short-term re-investment of excess operating funds.

Last-in, first-out (LIFO): A method of inventory valuation by which the inventory items are tracked in and out in date order. When a sale is made, it is the cost of the newest items in inventory that is applied to cost of goods sold account, and it is the cost of the oldest purchases that remain in inventory. Note that some taxation authorities do not allow this method. Check with your accountant.

Lease obligation: See **Capital lease obligations**.

Liability: Something that is owed by the business to outside parties. Liabilities can be current or long-term, depending on when the obligation is to be settled.

Limited liability company (LLC): A newer form of business ownership in the United States that carries with it characteristics of both a partnership and a corporation.

Limited liability partnership (LLP): A newer form of business ownership in Canada. Generally, it can be used only by professionals (accountants, lawyers, doctors). It has some benefit to the owners as it limits some of the normally unlimited liability of the partners.

Liquidity: The ability of an asset to convert into cash, or its ability to be easily sold. Assets are shown on the balance sheet in the order of their liquidity, the most liquid (cash) coming first.

Long-term liability: An obligation that is not expected to be settled within one year. The current portion of these liabilities (i.e., present value of payments due within one year) is shown in the current liability section of the balance sheet.

Lower of cost or market (LCM): A method of valuation usually applied only to inventories. Inventory must be recorded on the balance sheet at the lower value of its original cost or its value on the current market.

Management accounting: The accounting done internally to assist managers in their decision-making role. Management accounting encompasses budgeting, forecasting, unit costing, and ratio analysis.

Market value: See **Fair market value**.

Marketable securities: Investments (usually made with temporary excess operating funds) that are highly liquid, such as stocks, bonds, mutual funds, and income certificates. Marketable securities are presented on the balance sheet as current assets, as usually they will be converted to cash within one year.

Matching principle: One of the fundamental accounting principles that states that expenses should be matched to the revenues to which they relate.

Meals and entertainment: An important category of expenses, meals and entertainment usually attracts separate taxation treatment.

Mortgage payable: The balance of a business's debt that is secured by the business's real property. The most common reason for the borrowing is the purchase of land and buildings in which the business will operate. The present value of the mortgage payments due within one year are presented in current liabilities on the balance sheet, and the present value of the payments due more than one year out are presented in the long-term liability section.

MYOB. *Mind Your Own Business,* a popular accounting software program for small businesses.

Net book value: The difference between the original cost of a capital asset and its accumulated depreciation.

Net income: The income left in an accounting period after all expenses have been deducted from revenues. The term net income is used only if the revenues exceed the expenses.

Net loss: The deficit for an accounting period that occurs when the expenses for that period exceed the revenues.

Note receivable: An amount backed by a promissory note to be paid to a business.

Obsolescence: Usually used in reference to inventory, obsolescence is the loss in use of an item due to new and improved items taking its place, changes in customer preference, or other conditions unrelated to the physical condition of the item.

Operating activities: Those activities in which a business engages that create its main source of profit.

Operating cycle: The period of time it takes for a business to complete a full round of its operating activity. It is the time it takes to convert cash back into cash, which includes buying inventory, selling inventory, and collecting the receivables.

Owners' equity: The amounts owed by a business to its owners rather than outside parties.

Partnership: One of the three main forms of business ownership. A partnership is an unincorporated business with two or more owners. Partnerships are jointly owned by the partners and do not have a separate "legal life" of their own.

Periodic inventory: A method of accounting for inventory by which all purchases throughout the operating cycle are posted to cost of goods sold. Inventory is physically counted at the end of the period, and the adjustment for goods sold is made at that point. With this method, inventory is correct only at the end of the period.

Perpetual inventory: A method of accounting for inventory by which goods are recorded as being removed from inventory as they are sold. With this method, inventory is always theoretically correct and is checked against a physical count at the end of the period.

Posting: The process of summarizing general journal entries and recording them in the general ledger.

Preferred stock: Shares of a corporation that in the event of a dissolution of the corporation, entitle their holders to receive dividends and net assets of the corporation in preference to the common shares.

Prepaid expenses: Expenses that have been paid in the current period but which relate to future periods. Prepaid expenses appear as current assets on the balance sheet.

Profit: See **Net income**.

Profit and loss (P&L) statement: Another name for an income statement.

QuickBooks: A popular accounting software program for small businesses.

Residual value: The amount that a capital asset is expected to be worth at the end of its useful life with the corporation.

Retained earnings: The amount of cumulative net income that remains in the business that has not been paid out to the owners.

Revenue: The amount of net assets generated by a business as a result of its operations.

Service life: The period of time over which a capital asset is expected to be useful to a business.

Shareholder: An owner or internal investor of a corporation.

Simply Accounting: A popular accounting software program for small businesses.

Sole proprietorship: One of the three major forms of business ownership. A sole proprietorship is an unincorporated company owned by a single owner. It has no "legal life" of its own.

Solvency: The ability of a company to settle its liabilities with its assets.

Statement of cash flows: One of the three major financial statements. The statement of cash flows explains the changes in assets, liabilities, and net equity for the period.

Statement of changes in financial position: An older term for the statement of cash flows.

Stockholder: See **Shareholder.**

Straight-line depreciation: A method of calculating depreciation of capital assets that results in an even amount of depreciation being expensed every period.

Sum of the years' digits method (SYD): A seldom-used method of accelerated depreciation that results in more depreciation being expensed in earlier years.

Taxable income: The amount of net income that is subject to income tax. It will differ from net income per the financial statements by any differences between GAAP and tax regulations.

Transaction: A financial event that is recorded in a business's books.

Working papers: A set of documents prepared for the external accountants to verify the balances and calculations made in a business's books.

Writedown: An accounting entry to reduce the carrying value of an asset, such as inventory, to its market value.

Write off: A slang term for expensing a cost in the books of a business.